Playful Pottery

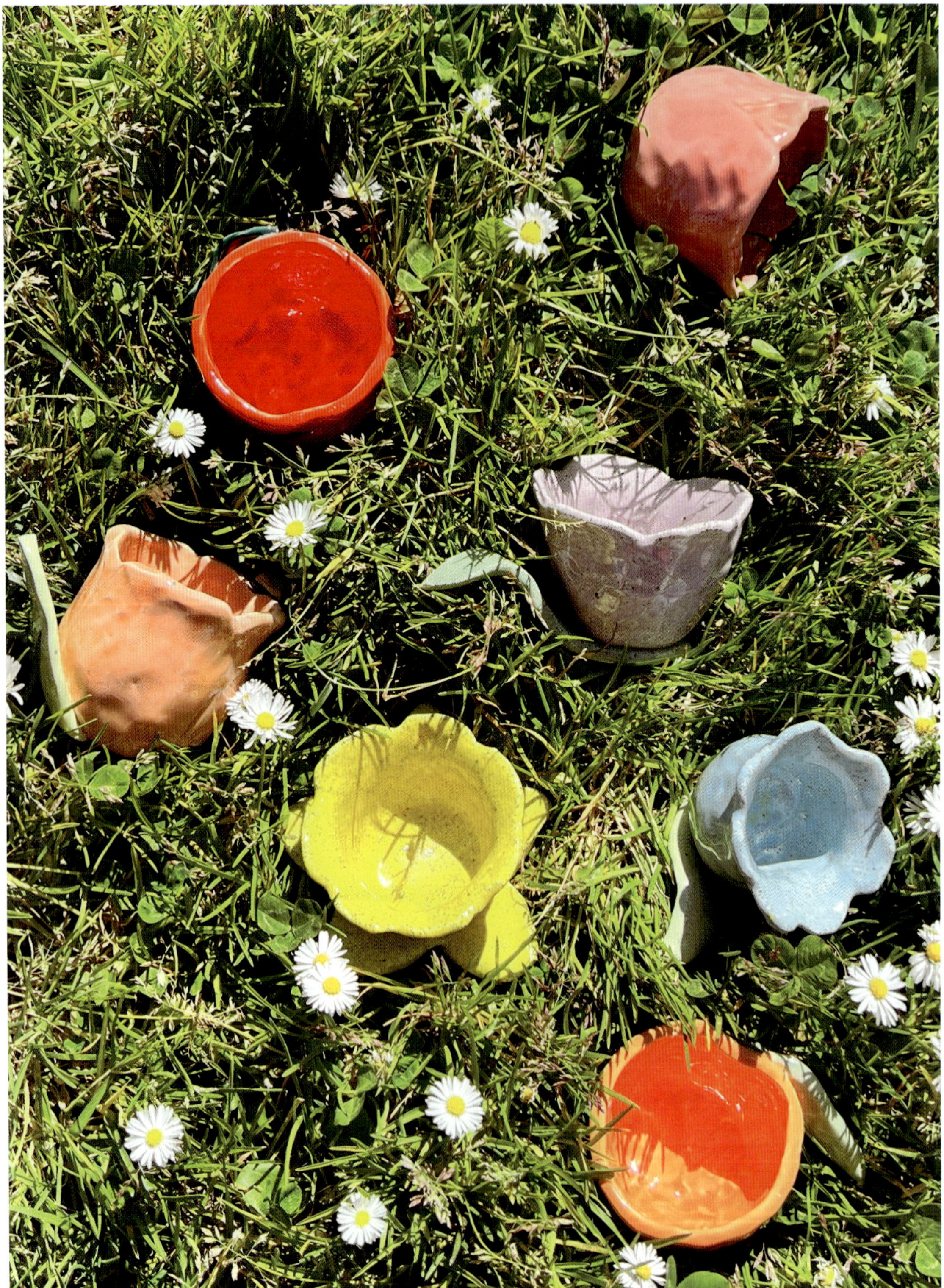

Playful Pottery

THE MUD WITCH'S GUIDE TO CREATING CURVY, COLORFUL CERAMICS

Viviana Matsuda

rockynook

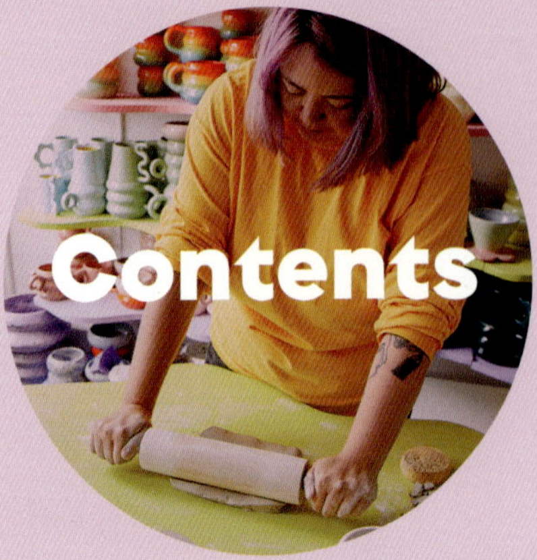

Contents

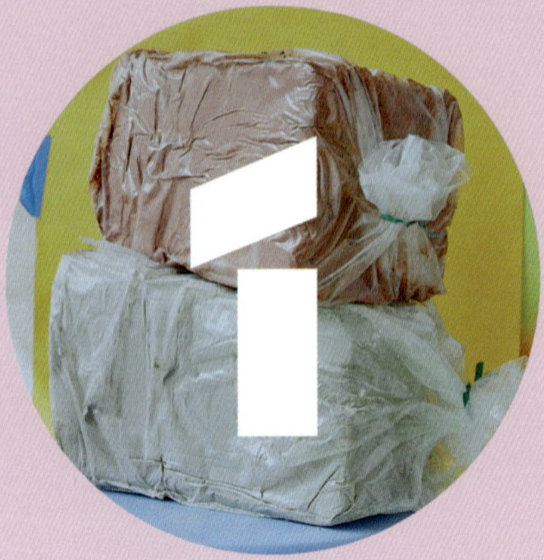

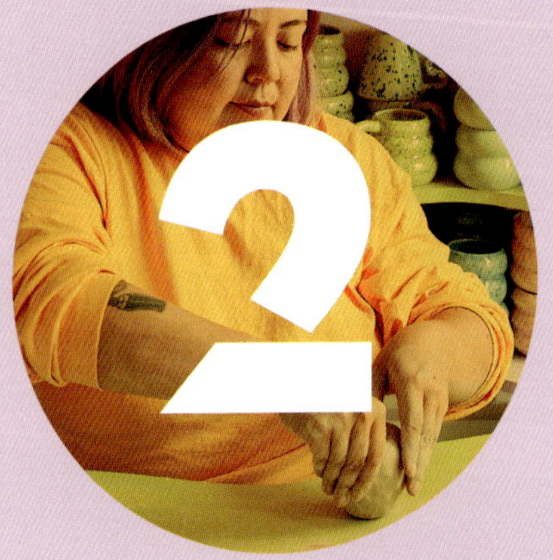

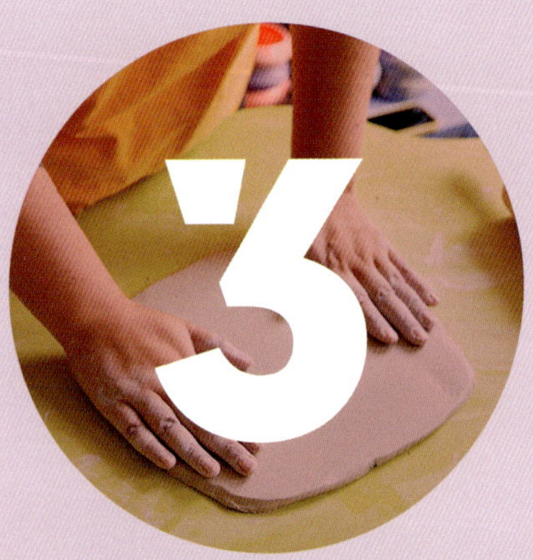

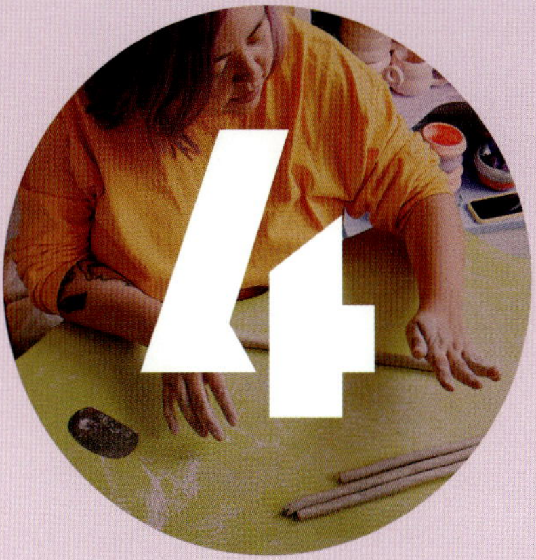
4

5

6

7

INTRODUCTION

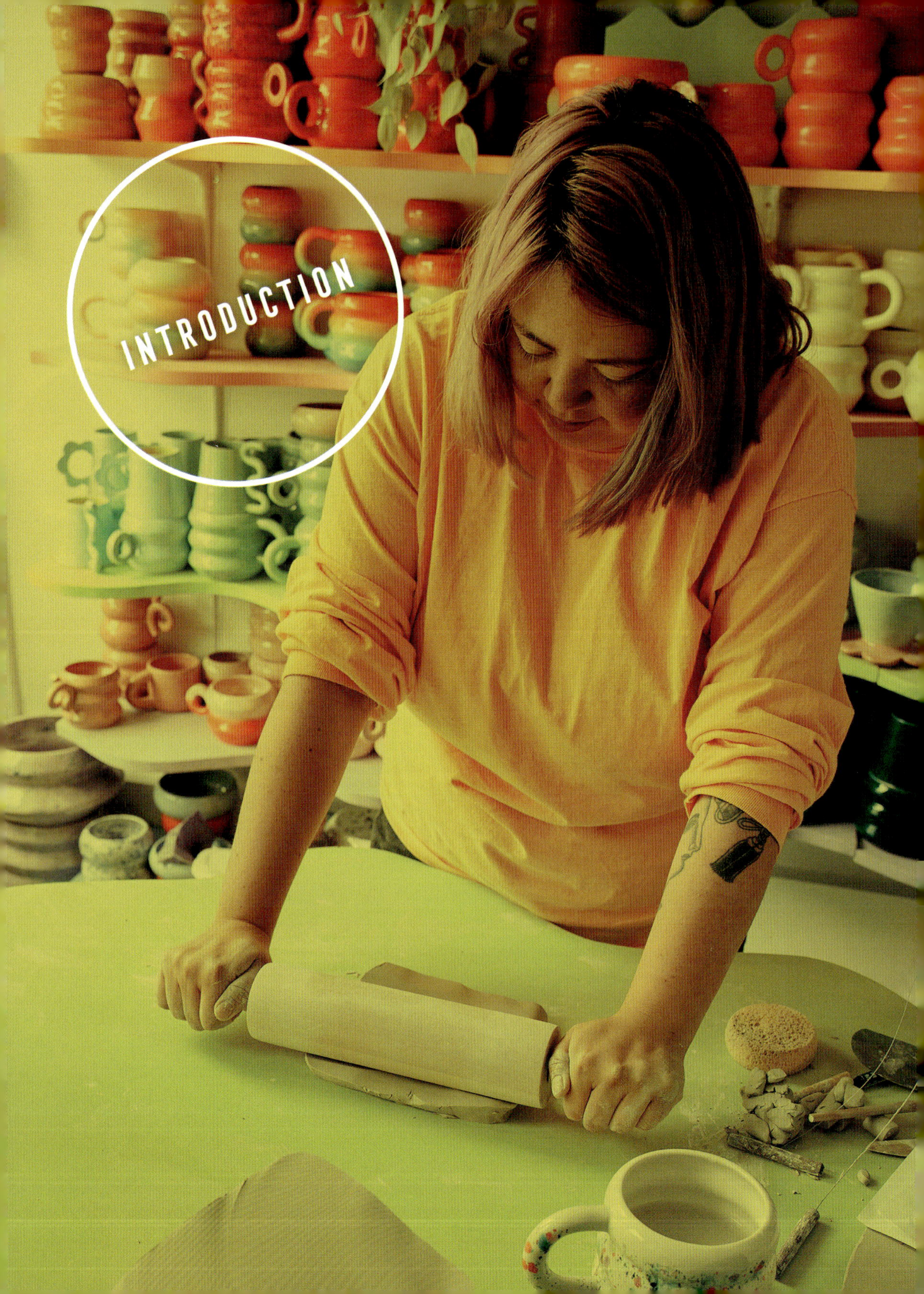

There's a reason making pottery feels like home. From our first tactile experiences as children forming mud pies, all the way to our ancestors making pottery, clay is a part of everyone's history. It brings us back to our childhoods where a mess was never to be questioned—your mess would always be justified by your creations. Clay up to your elbows and on your face—what a freeing feeling! When is the last time you've let go to that point? This is why the main focus of this book is to learn to enjoy the experience of working with clay rather than focusing on the products you create. Your final product could just be the amount of space you make for yourself to enjoy creating.

I wrote this book not only to share clay skills, but more importantly to teach people how to treat themselves when starting a creative endeavor. How do we manage our expectations? How do we treat ourselves while learning? How do we adapt when the unexpected happens?

We live in a capitalist society that tells us we aren't anything if we don't produce and if we don't squeeze every drop of our day into some sort of productivity, then we are wasting our time. We literally can't even relax without the pull of productivity. This "work hard, play hard" attitude needs to retire. Even the language of this saying is ridiculous. Why would I ever want to make life harder, especially at work or play? We must pay attention to how this attitude of productivity affects how we talk to ourselves. What has this attitude done to our creative selves and how we view experiences where productivity isn't the goal? With this book, I hope the reader will come away with a basic understanding of clay as well as a better understanding of their creative self.

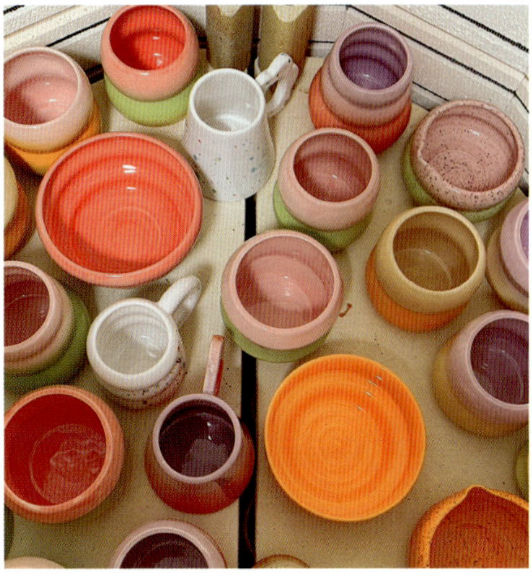

Finding Your Own Style

Finding your own style is important. It's the difference between expression and replication. Viewing things on Pinterest and replicating them can be tempting but here are some tips on how to admire other artist's works while respecting their work. Collect images that you love that aren't pottery. Yup, you heard me, this will help you define your aesthetic. Gather up the images you love and write down specifics on why they speak to you and what you like about them. When you record your findings, the description doesn't have to be in words. You could draw lines or shapes as long as you're not copying imagery. Is it the color, the mood, the motion, the shapes? Are they fun or regal? I always think writing things down is a great way to organize your thoughts. Once you have your list, you'll start noticing the similarities. Narrow them down and *voilà*! You have a foundation of your style. Now start your project with this list in your view.

Prepare Yourself to Create

Clay has taught me many things about patience and the importance of being kind to ourselves while we are learning. This kindness can be transferred to all aspects of our lives because we are all constantly learning no matter our age.

Being kind to yourself means more than the literal definition of the words. It also means taking the time to properly prepare yourself for success physically and emotionally. You will fail at some things, this is a fact, but it is also how you will learn to solve problems. Things might not turn out how you want them to. So, will you learn to love it or leave it? There is no shame in leaving it, by the way. There is no need to surround ourselves with failed projects just because we tried something that didn't work out and feel guilty not keeping it. If you don't love it, leave it. If it's greenware, repurpose the clay. If it's bisque, smash it and use it for drainage in your potted plants. If it has been fired, put a plant in it, donate it, or trade it. One person's unwanted piece could be another person's daily coffee cup. When I was first learning clay, at the end of each school year, the studio would have a big sale of all the donated unwanted pieces, and you wouldn't believe some of the things that were traded in. It's nice to see someone find beauty in a piece you didn't like because you were holding on to your expectation of the piece rather than the reality of it.

▶ For instructions on making this cute mini pool, see page 48.

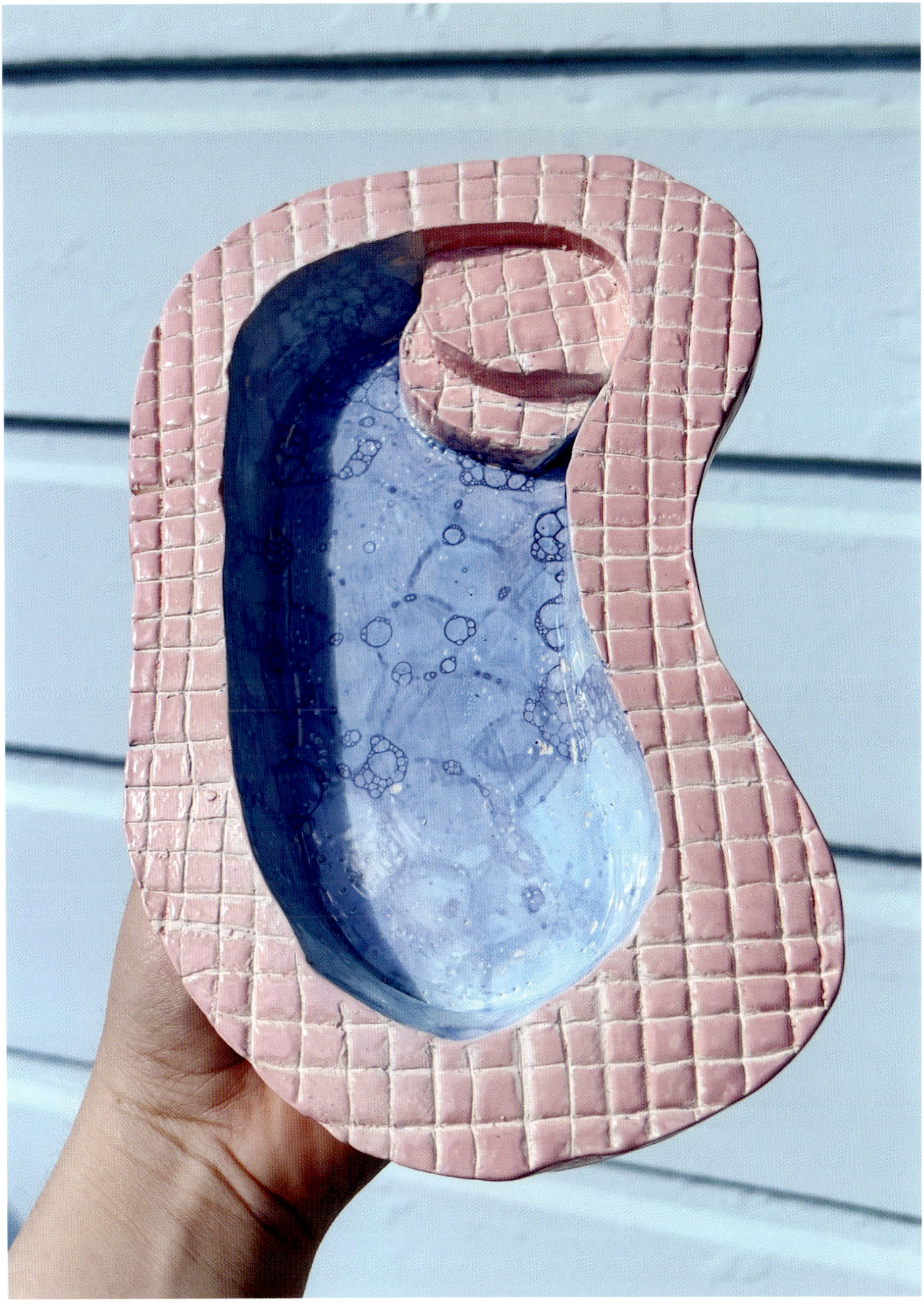

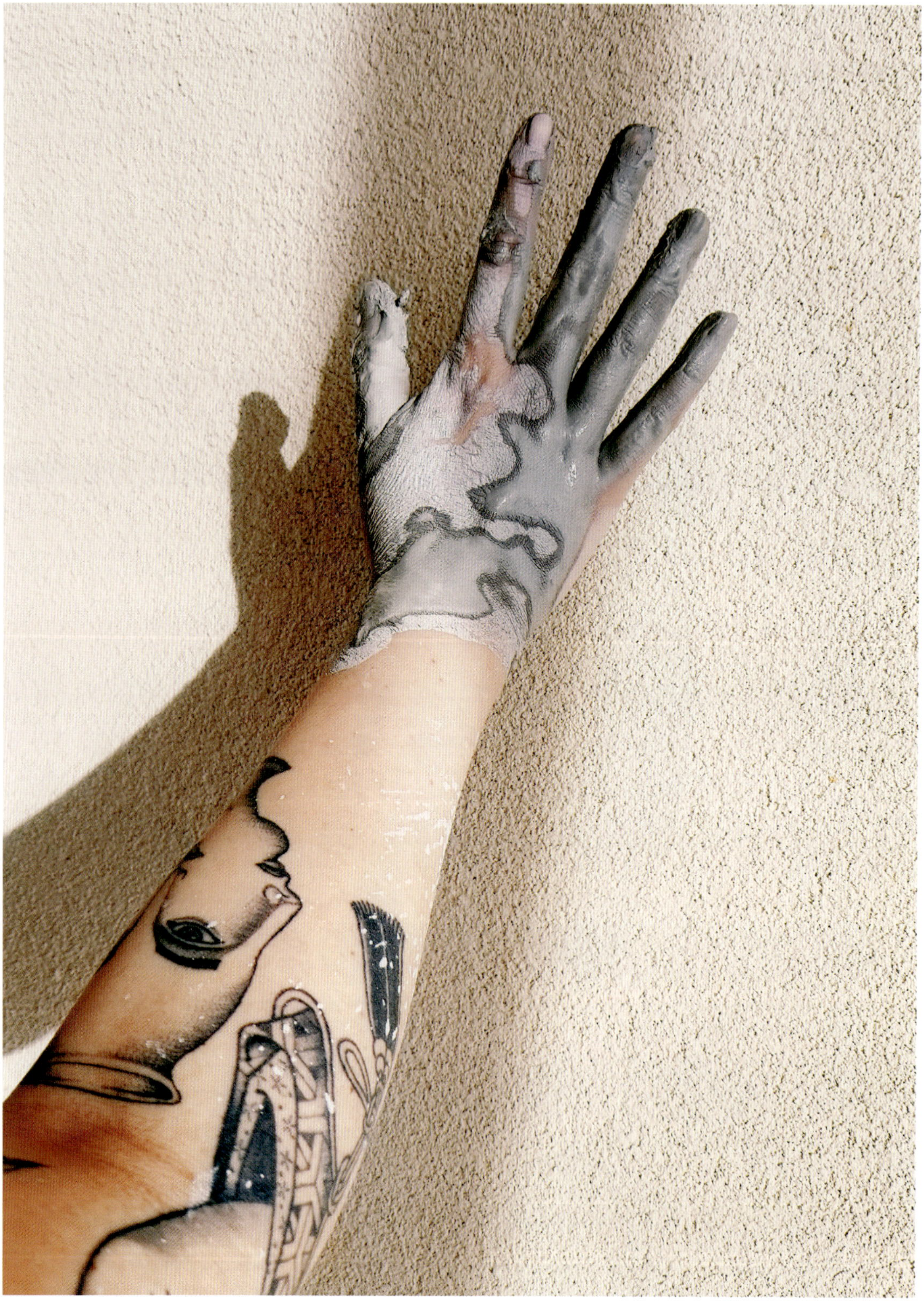

It is important to set realistic expectations. Will you become a clay master after a week? No. After a month? Not likely. Three months? Nope. A year? Three years? A decade? Eh, maybe. But there are those who have been working with clay for years and the only limit to their growth is their willingness to learn.

When starting out, pick a beginner's project that is realistic, or choose a project that is vague so you have space to pivot if things don't go exactly as planned. Starting with something small and simple like an espresso mug would be best. If the handle falls off the mug, then it becomes a cup! Is there a crack at the bottom? Sounds like a great container for a plant. Did your cup blow up in the kiln? Could make good terrarium gravel. Know that things will not always go as planned but it's how you respond that's important.

Stay Present with Your Work

It's important to stay present with your pieces. Focus on what it looks like now and move forward with it. Let go of past expectations, enjoy the present, and embrace the unexpected. When I was first throwing on the wheel there were times I would pull the walls of my cups a bit too far out. My instinct was to try to funnel the walls back in because I would be holding myself to the idea of making a uniform set of cups, rather than just accepting I had made a cup and a bowl. I would struggle as I tried to make the clay go beyond its capabilities—and beyond mine—as it eventually tore and folded from being overworked. The funny thing about clay is you work with it; it does not work for you. Working with clay is a partnership, and just like any other partnership, there are boundaries

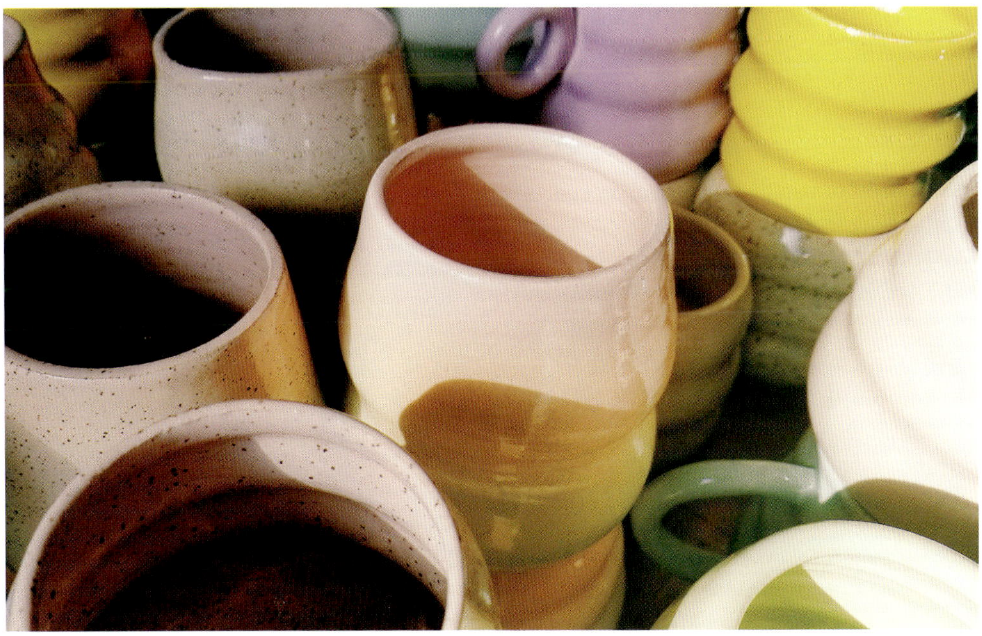

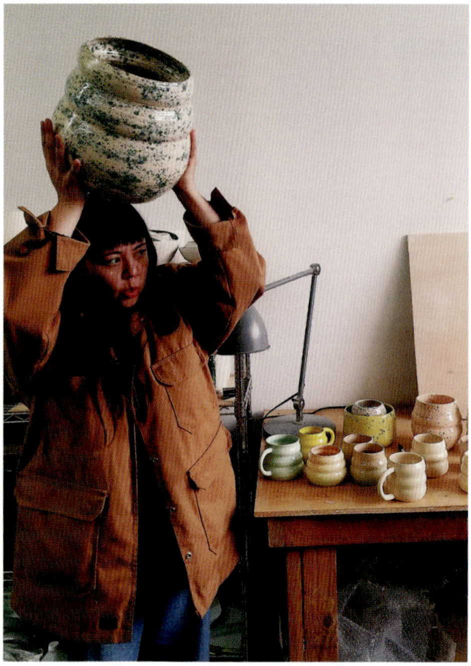

and limitations. Don't stress the clay out. It will protest if it is overworked and not respected.

Plan on no plan. Planning to have a day just to feel the materials and get to know them is essential. Plan a day of clay with no set goals. Such a meditative day will allow you to relieve yourself of the pressure of making something that has a purpose. We don't have to be making things for use all the time. Allow yourself time to simply play with the clay. Maybe you'll make something fun or maybe you'll end up with a big ball of clay. Even if you are learning to work with clay with the goal of starting a small business, this is still an essential step that shouldn't be skipped.

When I first started in clay, I really thought I would be a whiz at the wheel, and it was a humbling experience when the clay told me, "Nope." After the frustration of not "getting it" in the first two weeks, I thought maybe the wheel wasn't for me. I now realize I almost quit not because clay was too difficult but because my expectations were unrealistic. I wonder how much less hard on myself I would have been if I had told myself I would get better at the wheel in months rather than weeks.

How I Got Started

Starting a pottery business was never my plan. I always knew I would do something creative for a living, but I ended up going to school for product development in fashion. Sometimes we spend time on something only to discover it's not for us. I worked jobs when I was in my 20s that were just that, a job. As I was finding my way, I always had the support of my dad who would take me to the bookstore for creative inspiration. Then, suddenly, he got a cancer diagnosis. By late summer he was gone. He was a very creative person and liked working with his hands. He was a wheel thrower in his younger years and when he retired, he got into sculpting. After he passed, we had to clean out his studio and my mom asked what we should do with all his supplies. I thought there would be no better time to dive into a craft, so I signed up for a class at Laney College in Oakland. I soon found myself in the studio five days a week. Pottery became my stress relief. Too much stress made too much pottery, and the small apartment I shared with my partner became filled to the brim. So, with my partner's encouragement/complaining, I decided to post some pieces for sale and that's how the Mud Witch business began!

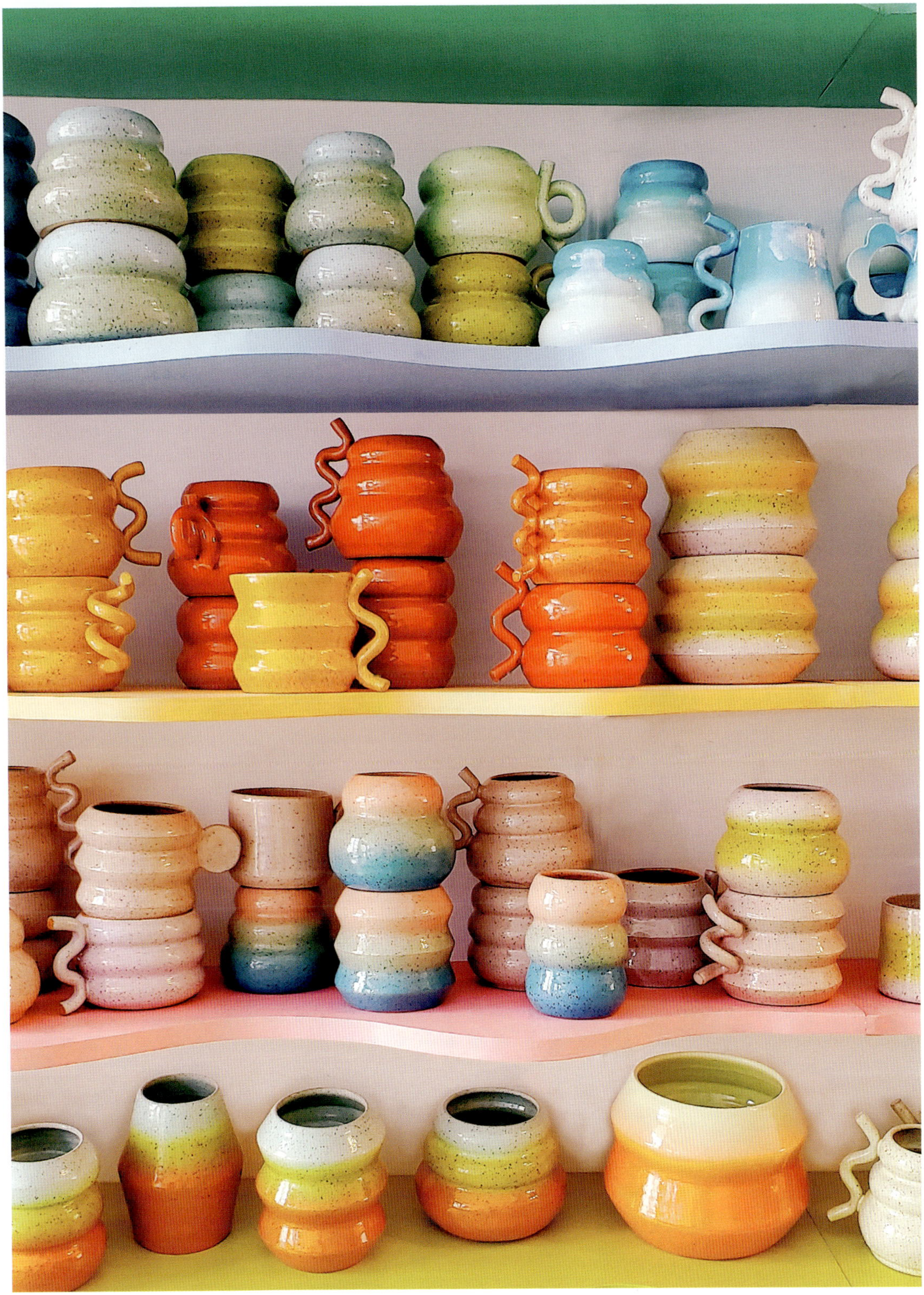

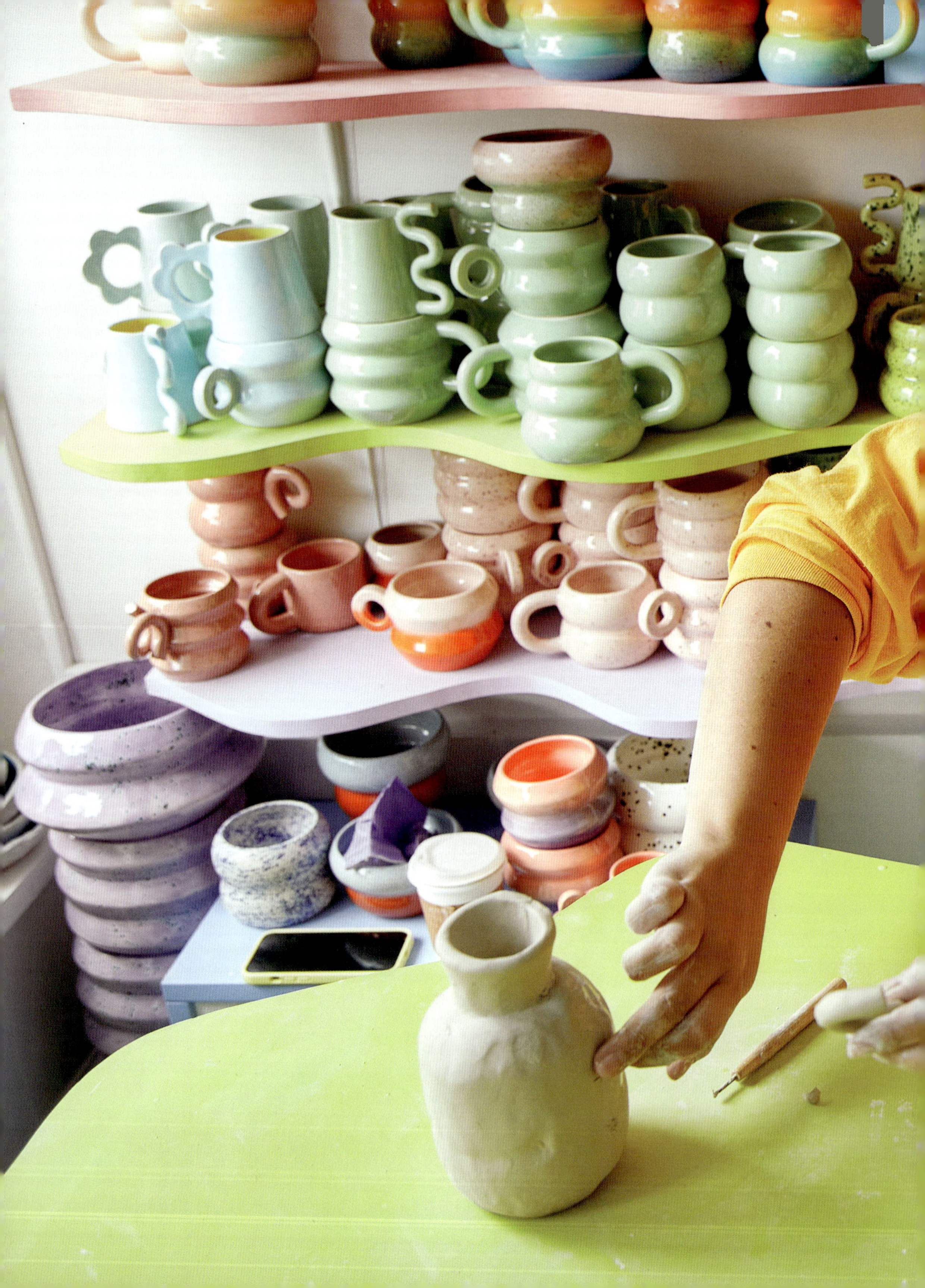

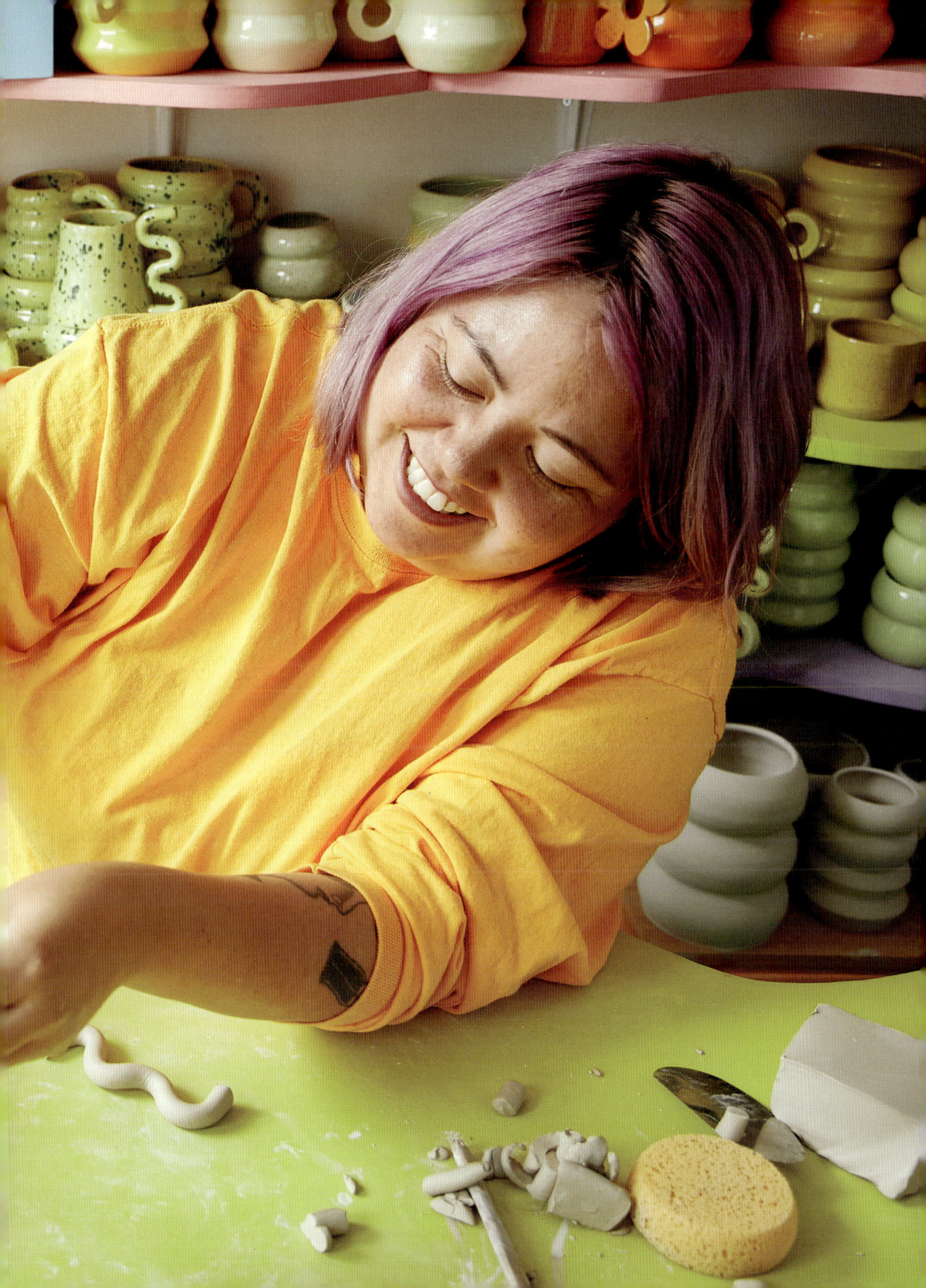

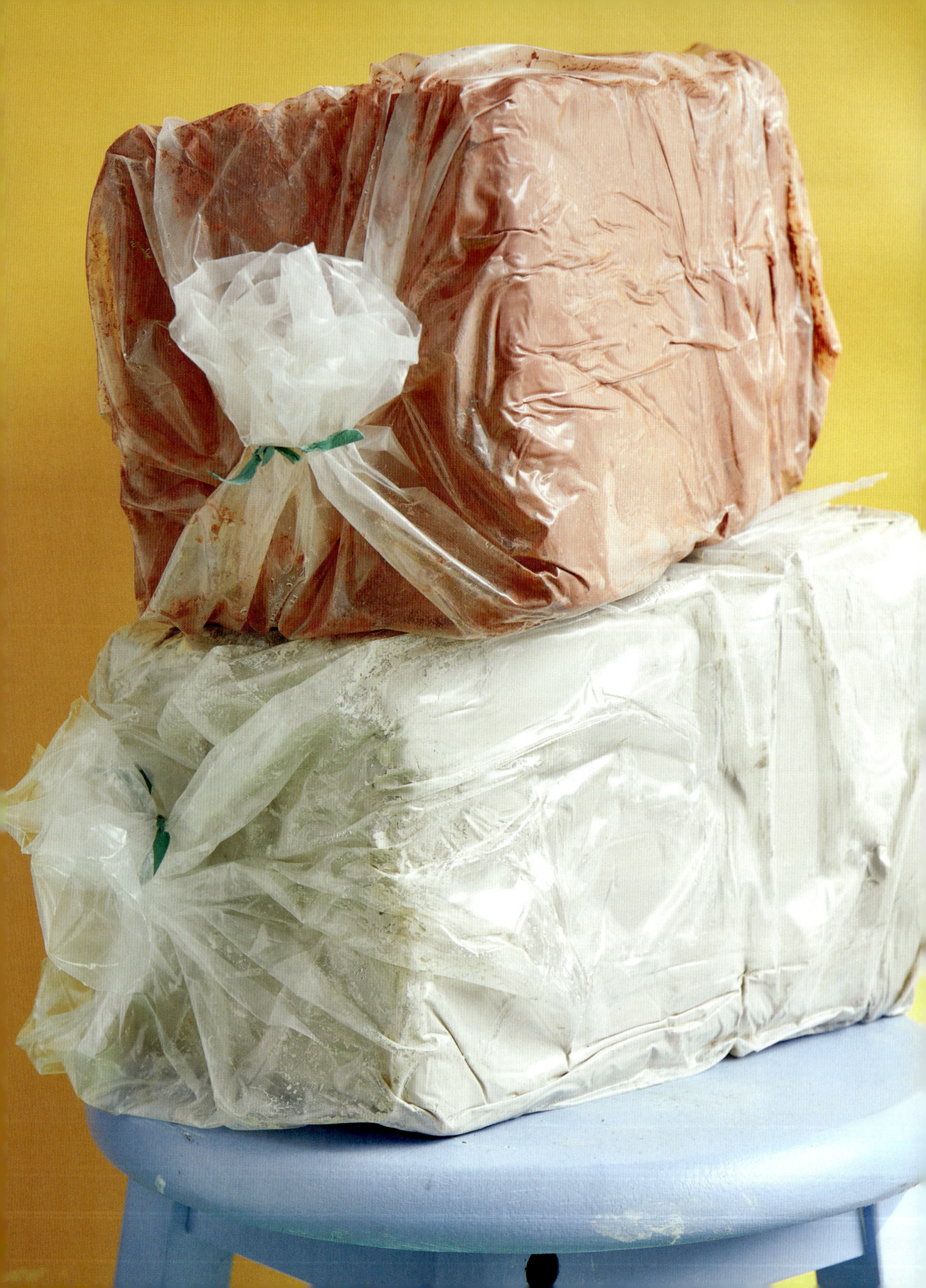

Get to Know the Materials

TYPES OF CERAMICS
PAGE 15

GETTING TO KNOW THE CLAY
PAGE 15

GETTING TO KNOW THE TOOLS
PAGE 20

FINISHED CERAMICS
PAGE 20

CHAPTER 1

Get to Know the Materials

Clay is composed of eroded granite minerals, silica, and alumina mixed with water. Does that mean clay is old rock? Yup. This erosion process is natural and can be found everywhere. I've gone on hikes near Lake Merritt in Oakland, California and have found clay deposits. The interesting thing is that when you're firing clay you are kind of bringing clay back to stone, hence the name "stoneware." What is stoneware, you ask? Let's dive into some basics!

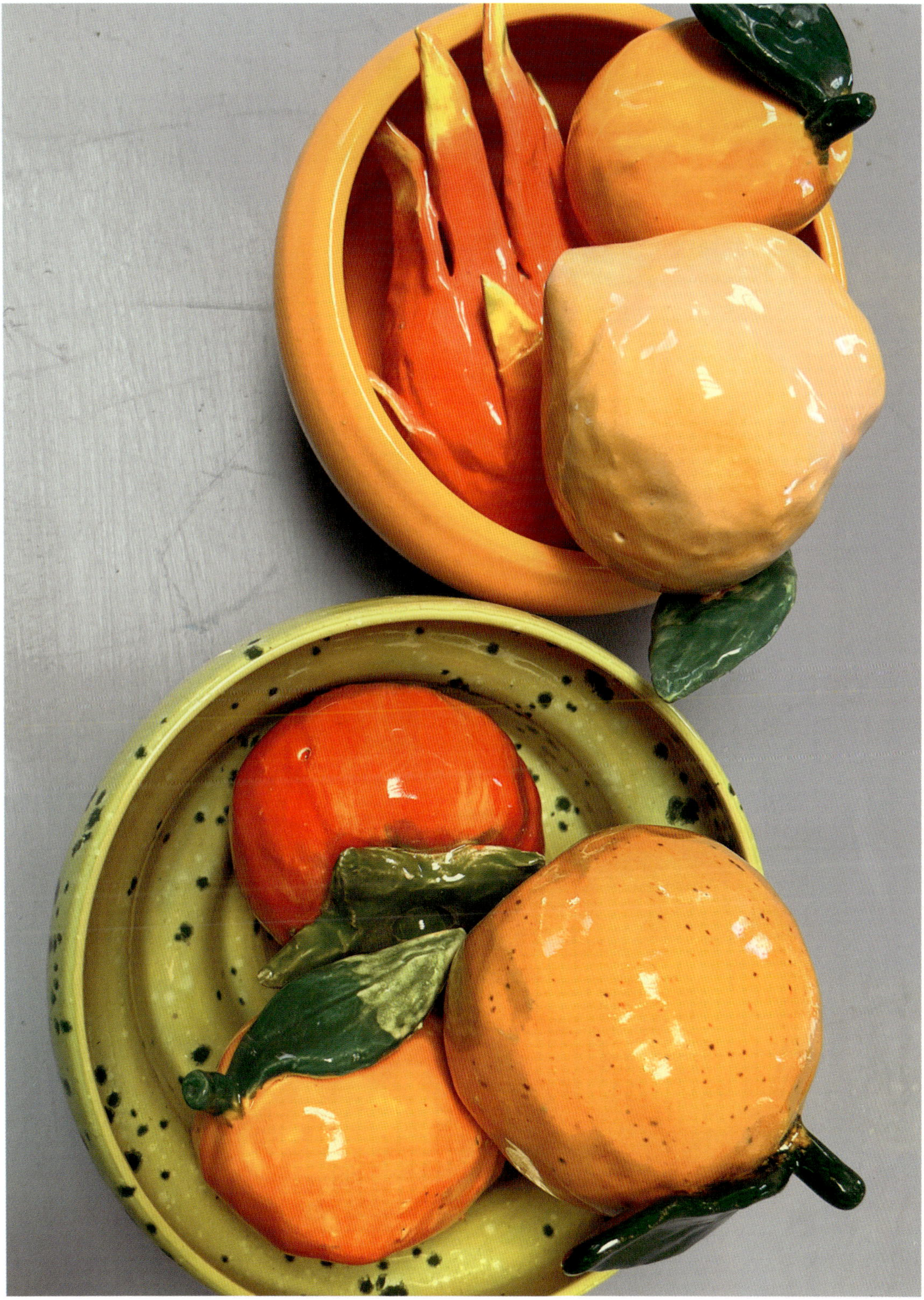

A

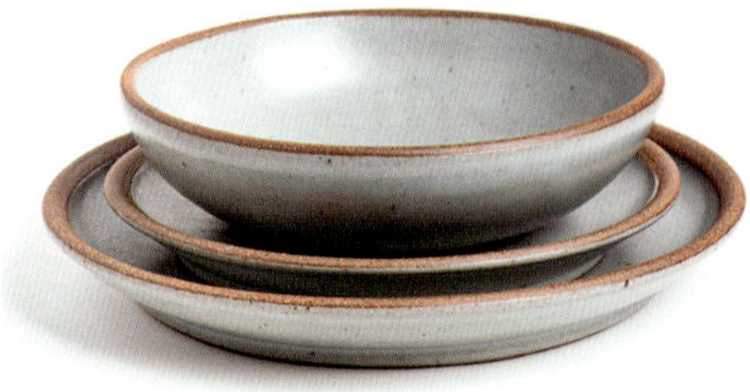

B

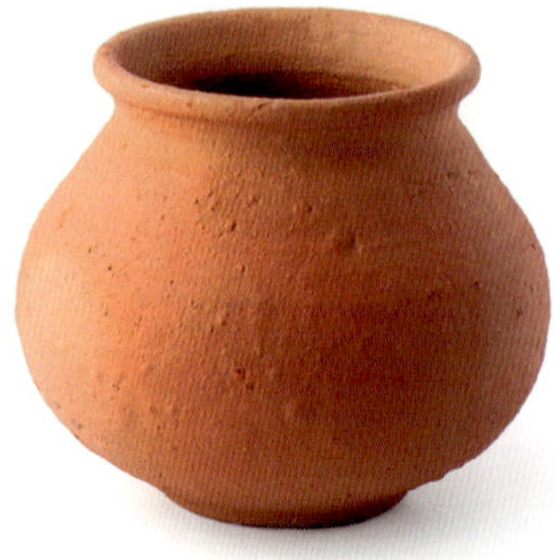

C

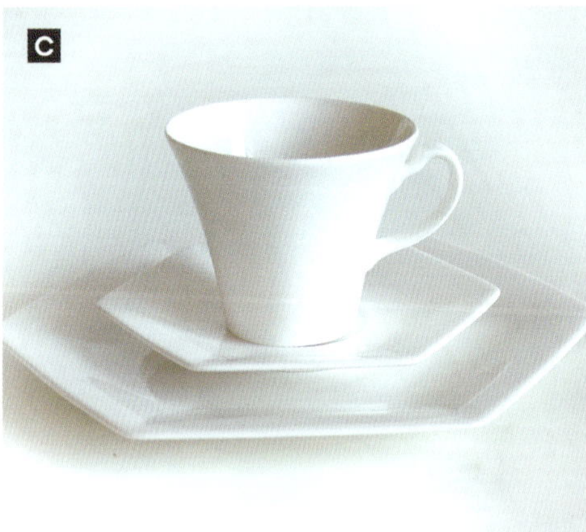

D

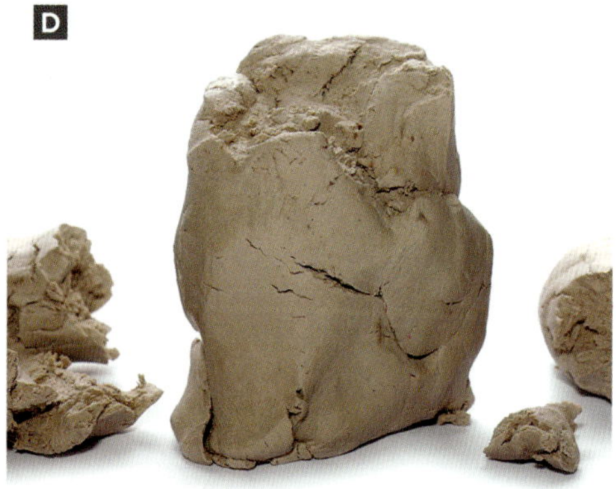

E

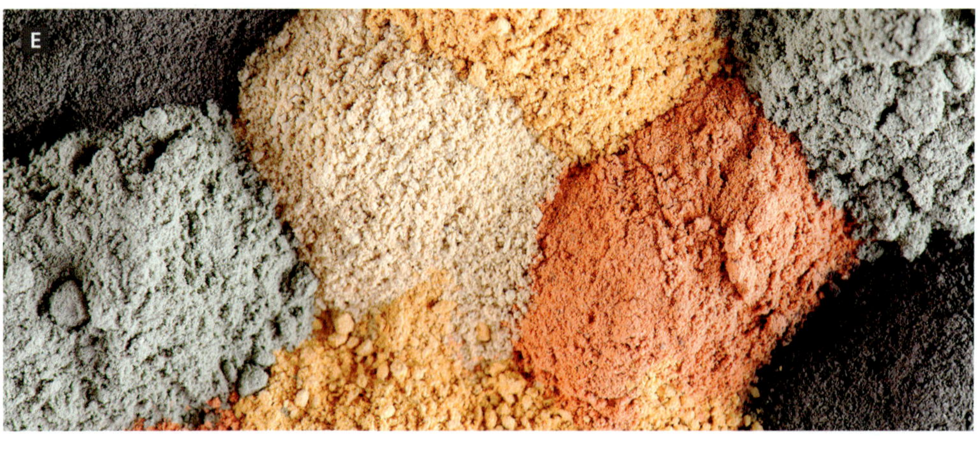

Types of Ceramics

Ceramic pieces are made from clay and water that are shaped into desired forms. Let's look at the most common types of ceramics.

A **Stoneware** is a broad term for clay that has been fired at high temperatures to the point that it becomes vitrified and is no longer porous so it can hold water. This is the case with ceramic tableware.

A good example of **earthenware** **B** is the terracotta pots found at a garden store. These pots are fired at a lower temperature than stoneware and, generally, the lower the temperature a piece is fired the more delicate it is, therefore, you'll find that your terracotta flowerpots tend to chip easily. Generally, earthenware is fired at temperatures between 1,800- and 2,000-degrees Fahrenheit.

C **Porcelain** can be fired at very high temperatures. Porcelain clay is usually white and can be thrown to extremes. Some people throw this clay so thin that light can shine through it like a lamp.

D **Clay** can also contain other ingredients like iron, calcium, and potassium **E**.

Getting to Know the Clay

There are many types of clays, and each has its own personality. Some are sandy and cooperative, and some are smooth, moody, and unforgiving. You must find which works best with you. Again, *the clay works with you not for you*. What are you willing to work with? For example, porcelain is beautiful but unforgiving and moody. Soldate 60 is rustic, easygoing, and flexible. Every clay is different, so try out a few and see what works. See below for more details on what clays work best for certain projects.

CLAY HAS MEMORY

When selecting a type of clay for a specific project it is important to keep in mind that clay has memory. If you're doing a slab building project for a more geometric shape, you would pick a clay that has some structure and isn't super fickle like porcelain. This is not to say you can't slab build with porcelain, but it will be more difficult than other clays.

When you roll out slabs and move them, they'll "remember." What does this mean? If you roll a slab and then drape it over your arm to move it, the clay will remember the shape it was in. If you're making a cube, the clay will remember the curve of your arm which will cause warping and cracking later in the process. It's best to keep the clay as flat as possible when moving it around, so picking a less flexible clay would be a better choice. A lot of sculptors use clay that's formulated with small fibers in it to keep it from breaking.

Giving the clay proper respect and acknowledging its boundaries will provide the foundation of a good relationship. Just like any other relationship, you should choose a counterpart as is. Don't try to change who they are!

Following are some types of clays and their "personalities." Clay varies from store to store and from region to region.

Speckled buff: Accommodating, flexible, and easygoing with attachments (such as handles on a mug).

Porcelain: Beautiful, takes color well, temperamental, and unforgiving.

Bmix: A middle-ground type that requires more attention with attachments than speckled buff. This is a great starter clay.

There are many different types of clays that are not listed here but these are my favorites.

PLAYING WITH THE MATERIAL

Sit with the clay and play with it, making sure your first interactions have no intentions of making anything. Run your fingers over the top. Does the clay roll over or flake or just make impressions? Think how this will affect smoothing out attachments. Squeeze the clay. Is it firm? Is it super flexible? Does it crack easily? This will affect how you form the clay. Add a splash of water. Does some of the clay separate the grog? Does the water make it easier or harder to work with the clay?

When I first got into clay, I preferred unglazed pieces because the beauty of the clay would be shown rather than covering it with a glaze. Clay comes in many different shades and textures, and when fired it can bloom into the unexpected. Some clays that look ashy gray before firing will be transformed into a gorgeous, richly speckled beach sand after it's fired. Some clays will start out as soft tan and then when fired will turn into the deepest beautiful brown.

LET'S TALK ABOUT SHRINKAGE

Clays shrink—some as much as 20 percent. The shrinkage rate will be labeled on the clay. Generally, the higher the firing temperature the more it shrinks due to the vitrification process. When I was just starting in hand building at the studio, I was firing at the highest temperature, so all of my pieces came out far smaller than I thought they would. I would make things I thought would be cups but by the time all the firings would be finished the "cups" were more like shot glasses. When making a piece, keep in mind that it will shrink as the clay dries out. Some folks who work in dry weather will actually hood their pieces with a sheet of plastic so they will have longer to work with it at its current state of moisture.

So, your piece is shrinking while you're making it and then it shrinks when it is drying. Then you bisque it in the first firing, which causes it to shrink some more because the clay particles are being fused together. After the bisque, you glaze it and then fire again the final time and it shrinks even more. By the end, you'll find your piece at a fraction of its original size. Keep this in mind when making functional items like mugs and dishes. We will discuss more about the firing process later in the book.

STAGES OF CLAY

Let's discuss the various stages of clay as it's formed into a piece.

Wet clay/plastic: This is the most malleable stage of clay when it's a solid. Fresh out the bag, this clay is easy to form with your hands and is a great stage to make pinch pots.

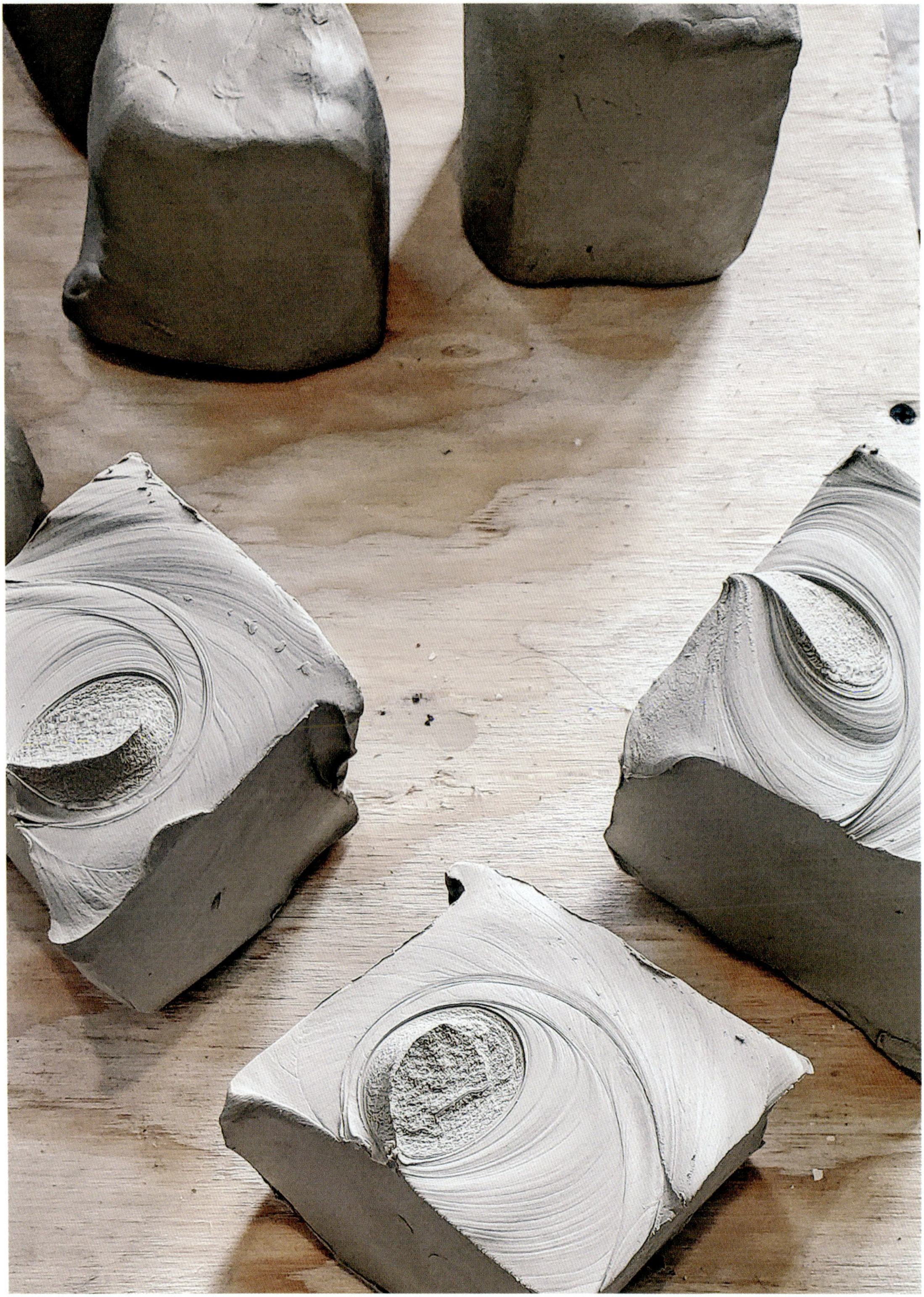

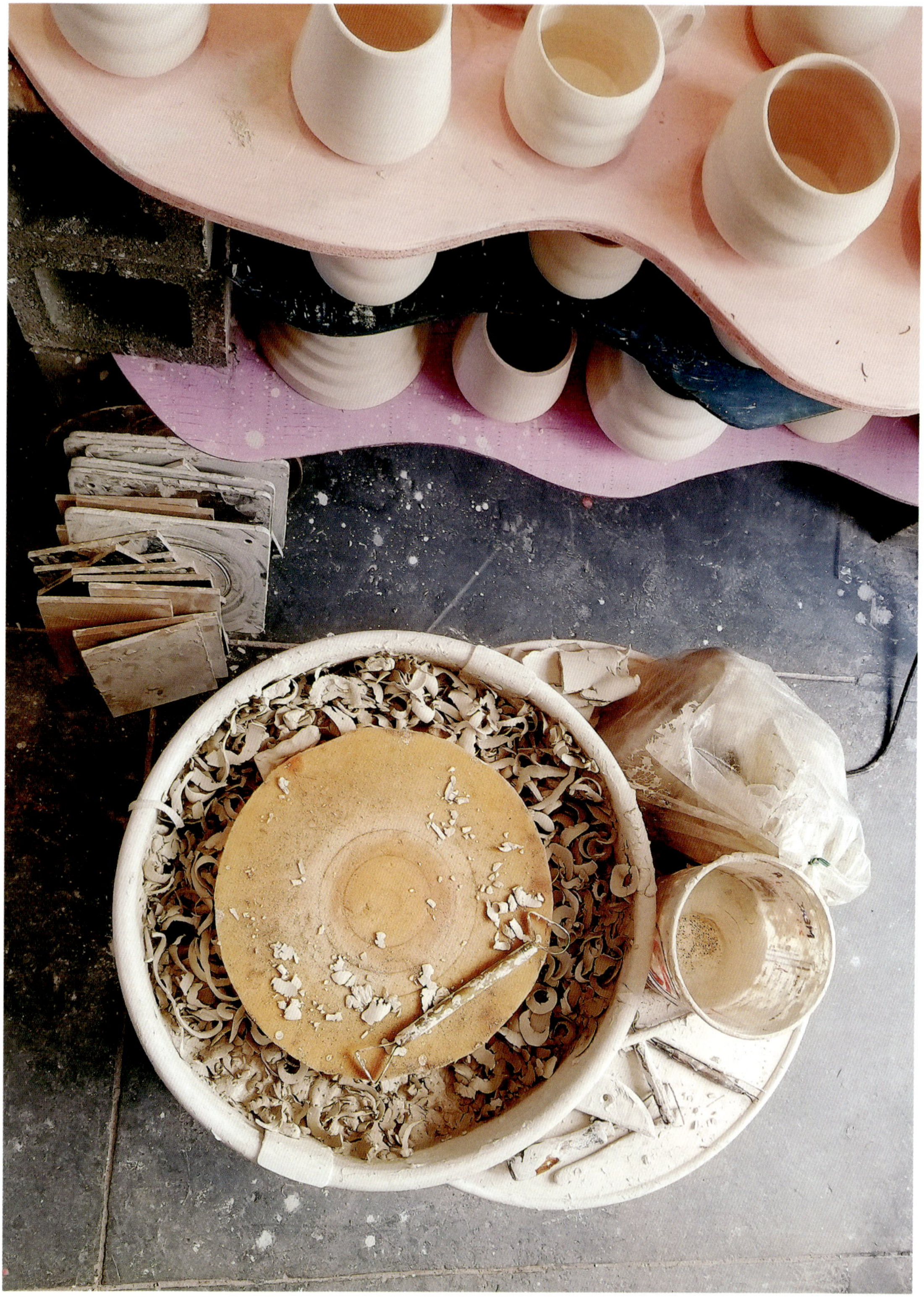

Leather-hard clay: Leather hard is a good stage for creativity. At this stage, the clay has lost enough moisture that it has just become stiff. This is the ideal stage for slab building and for adding attachments like handles. This is also a great stage for sgraffito. Sgraffito in pottery is when you brush colored slip onto your piece, let it dry for a bit, and then carve decoratively into the piece exposing the clay body underneath.

Bone dry/greenware: At this stage, the clay has dried completely but has not yet been fired. No attachments can be added nor can changes be made. The clay should look visibly dry and dusty in color. By this stage, it has shrunk a bit too. You should not try to rewet the clay. If you try to rewet at this stage, it could cause cracks to appear. Cracks in greenware are very hard to fix. Cracks expand and torque when they're in the kiln so if it's a little baby crack now it will become a big crack after it's fired. Also, don't expect to fill the crack with glaze or slip, as that would make it worse. If you see a crack, assess the situation. If it's a through and through crack, the piece might now be a planter with a drainage crack. If it's a crack on the rim it might have become a one-sided vase. If it's a surface crack that's not on the edge, you can try to carve and sand it out. There are special mixes you can buy to try and remedy cracks, but you could also repurpose the clay. Once the clay is bone dry and before it's been fired, it is as delicate as a potato chip. Don't carry your piece by the rim. Always use both hands to support it and be very careful with your attachments: a gentle knock or setting your piece down too hard can knock them off. Once your piece is bone dry it's ready for the first firing.

Bisqueware: This is fired greenware, usually low-fired. It will be strong enough to handle but still delicate and porous, which will make glaze easy to stick to the piece. At the bisque stage you can glaze and sand imperfections. Always wear lung protection when sanding and use the wet sanding technique. This is the first of two firings.

HOW TO WET SAND

Grab a bowl of water and some fine-grit sandpaper and head outside. Dip the sandpaper in the water and sand your problem area. Make sure the area you are sanding stays moist. You can use a spray bottle to get in crevasses. Wet sanding prevents particles from getting in the air, which could cause lung problems. Be sure to wear an N95 mask or respirator when sanding. *Please read the safety portion of this book on page 27.*

Make sure your piece is bone dry before its bisque firing. If there is still moisture in your piece when you do a bisque firing, it could cause the piece to explode or break. How can you tell if your piece is bone dry? The piece will look visibly dry and dusty. Check the bottom of the piece by flipping it gently. If you see a little dark spot in the center, that is moisture, which means it needs to dry longer. The bottom is the hardest part to dry because, generally, it is the thickest part of the piece and it gets the least air circulation. You can elevate pieces on a rack to help the foot dry faster. Another way to test if a piece is bone dry is if it's cool to the touch, it needs more time to fully dry.

Getting to Know the Tools

After familiarizing yourself with the clay you are using, start getting to know your tools. Keep note of how they interact with the clay. Pulling through it or cutting, dry or wet; pay attention to how the tools work with your clay.

HAND BUILDING TOOLS

The basic tool kit for hand building includes the following:

A Needle tool: Used for many things, including scoring, poking holes, cutting rims off pieces on the wheel, etc.

B Fettling knife: Cuts clay without dragging it.

C Sponge: Great for smoothing out and removing water.

D Cutting wire: A wire with two handles held tightly to cut through clay.

E Metal rib: Used to scrape the surface of clay.

CLAY TOOLS FOR THROWING

If you're throwing clay, the following tools are needed in addition to the list above:

F Wood rib: Used to compress clay walls on the wheel or to compress clay inside of pieces.

G Loop tool: Used for trimming pieces and for decorative carving.

H Ribbon tool: Used to trim bulk off the foot.

I Calipers: Used to measure pieces on the wheel.

J Chuck: Used to elevate pieces that have narrow necks so you are able to trim the foot.

SLAB BUILDING TOOLS

If you are slab building you will need the hand building tools above, along with the following:

K Rolling pin: Great for rolling out slabs but they need to be unfinished wood.

L Wooden boards: Used to move slabs without bending them.

M Plastic sheets: Used to cover pieces and slow down the drying process (also used for coil building).

COIL BUILDING TOOLS

If you are coil building, you will need the hand building tools above, along with the following:

N Paddle: Unfinished wood paddle to help shape pieces.

Finished Ceramics

After your bisque piece comes out, glaze it and do your final firing. Once your piece is fired in its glaze firing you've finally created pottery! Your finished pieces should give you some satisfaction. You should be proud of anything you made even if you don't keep it. It required a lot of work! If there are imperfections in the glaze, you can always reglaze and refire your piece. You can refire a piece an unlimited number of times; however, every

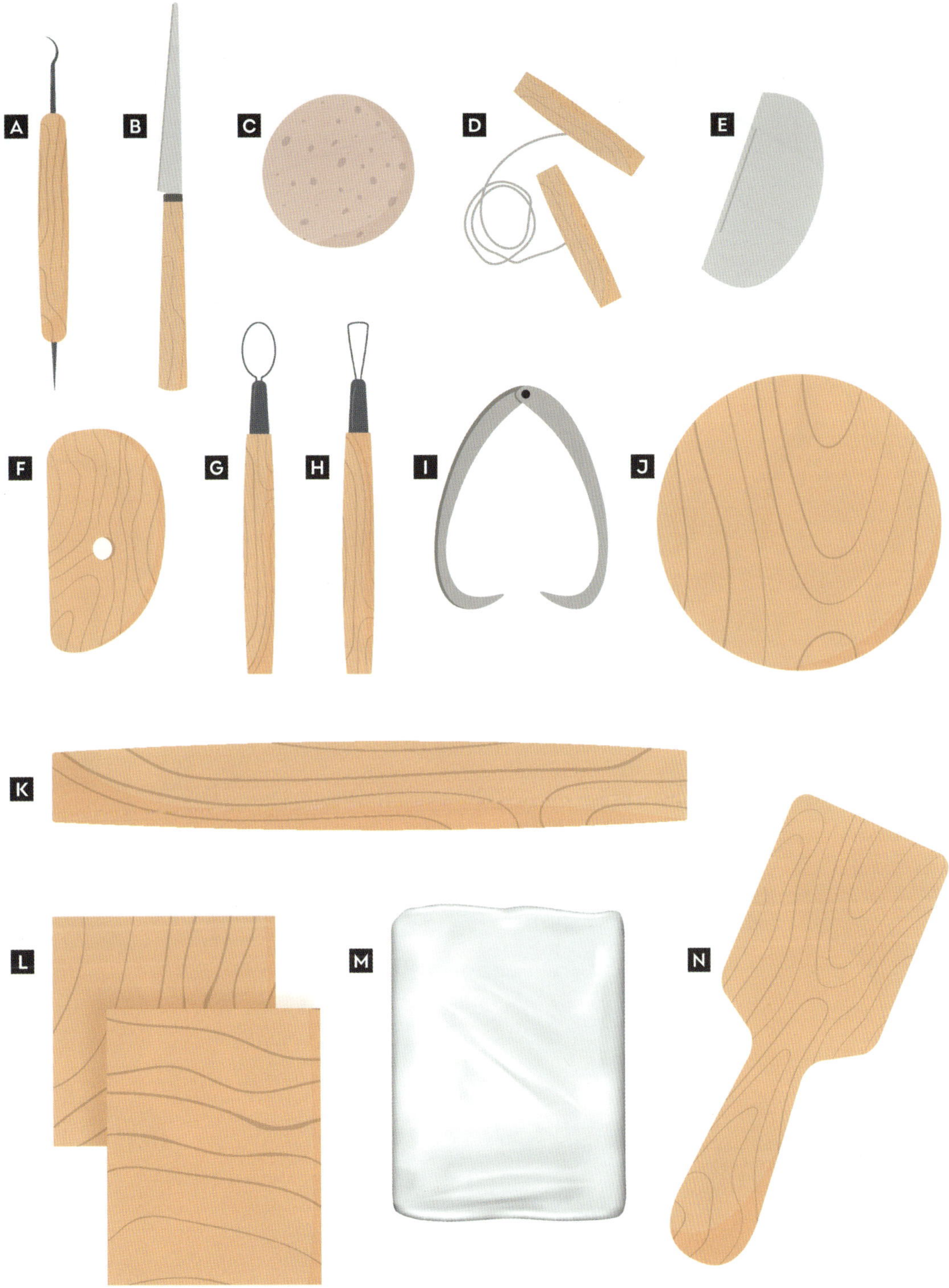
A
B
C
D
E
F
G
H
I
J
K
L
M
N

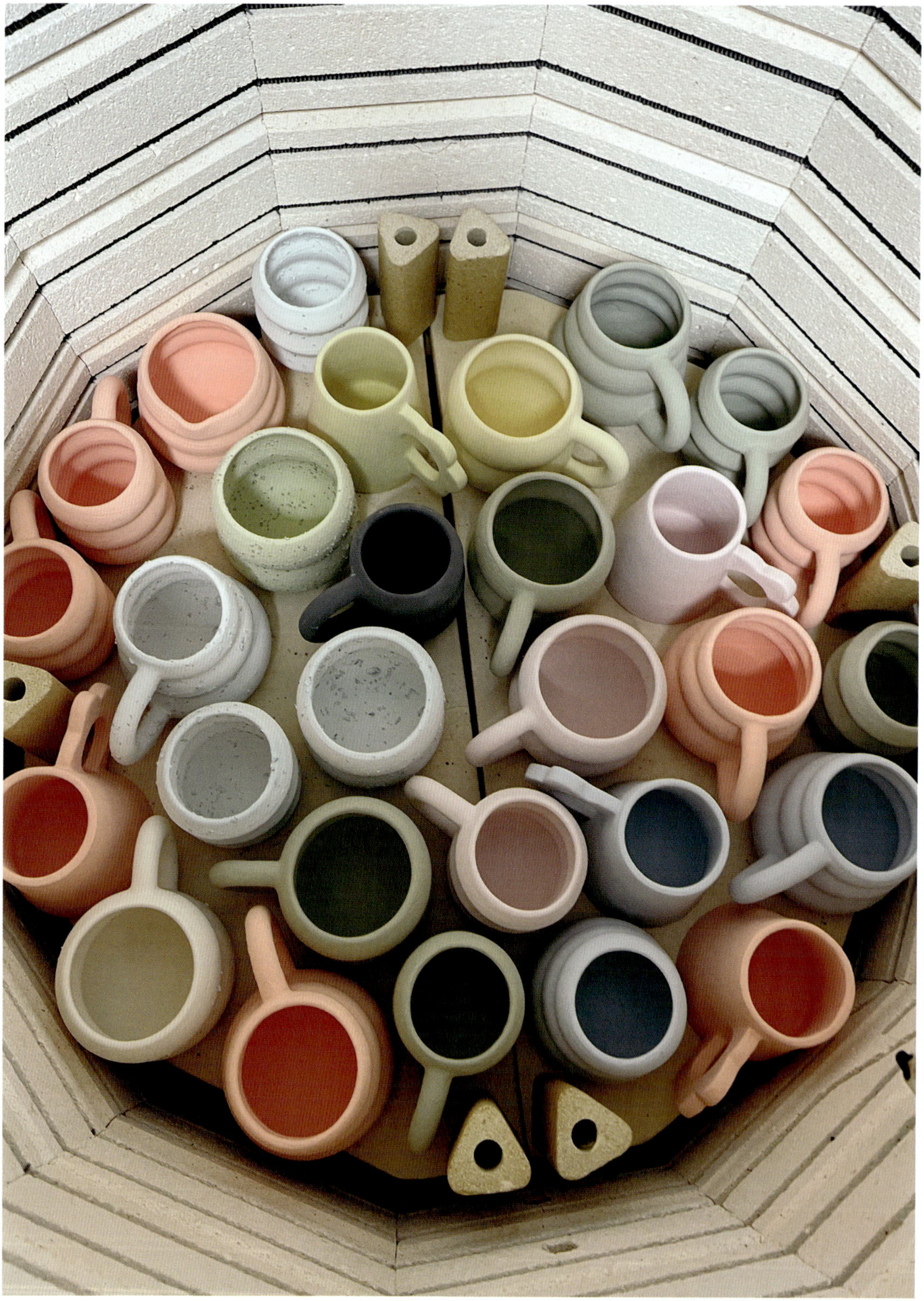

layer adds to the thickness of glaze on the piece, which can cause glaze to run.

KEY TERMS

Grog: Crushed, unglazed ceramics that are added to the clay. It generally feels a little chunkier than the rest of the smooth clay. Grog is added to clay to increase its strength. Grog looks similar to sand.

Pottery: Clay becomes pottery after the moisture is removed and the pieces have been vitrified in the kiln furnace during firing.

Glaze running: This is when the glaze drips down off the piece onto the kiln shelf, which damages the shelf. Kiln shelves aren't cheap and running glaze will cause your piece to be ruined as well as stuck to the shelf, which will take some elbow grease to clear off. Glaze running happens if you apply too much glaze, apply the wrong cone temp glaze, or could just be caused by the characteristic of the glaze. Having too much glaze is easy to do when you dip glaze. Refer to the instructions on the glaze for how long you should dip your piece, but generally do not go longer than three seconds. It's easy to get distracted and dip longer than three seconds, but when you wipe the foot, you'll notice the thickness of the glaze. If the glaze looks too thick, you can wash it off and start again, but be sure to wait a full day for the bisque to dry before you glaze it again. If the piece is still wet, the glaze might not stick to it.

Applying the wrong cone temp glaze for your firing is a big no-no. If you glaze a piece with low-fire glaze in a high-temperature firing, it will completely melt down the piece, ruining it and possibly ruining the shelves in the kiln as well. On that note, if you apply a high-fire glaze to a low-fire piece and fire it low, the glaze will not mature properly and will likely be matte, flaky, and definitely not food safe.

Kiln: A furnace or oven used for firing pottery.

Fire/firing: The process of heating glazes and clay to high temperatures to make it into pottery. Remember, clay is fired, not baked!

Kiln shelf: Kiln shelves are a part of the kiln furniture kit. The shelf is where your pieces lay in the kiln when being fired. They generally come in one-piece or half shelves and can be stacked at different levels. Kiln shelves go through a lot. They go through all the firings as well as being chipped away from glaze drips. You should check the health of your kiln shelves often; sometimes they can warp, which can then lead them to crack mid firing. To prevent this, place posts so that the balance of the weight of the shelf is even. Think about it like if you had a three-legged table. You wouldn't put two legs close to each other or on one side, you'd want the legs evenly apart.

Kiln post: Kiln posts are a part of a kiln furniture kit. They come in different sizes and different shapes, and are what hold up the kiln shelves. They can be stacked together to make a taller post if needed. They are basically the legs of a three-legged table. Yes, three legs and only three. Three posts are what make the most balanced shelf—not four.

Kiln furniture: Kiln furniture consists of a collection of shelves and posts that are used inside the kiln during firing. The furniture kits are different for each kiln and the potter's preferences.

Kiln wash: Kiln wash is a substance applied to a kiln shelf to protect the shelf. It basically adds a brittle barrier layer over the shelves so that if glaze drips, you can chip away that layer without damaging the shelf, but it has its limits.

Bisque firing: This is the first firing of clay after it has reached its driest stage (bone dry). The piece needs to be bisque fired so it will be stiff enough to be handled while glazing. Bisque firing also burns off impurities in the clay that can affect the color of your glaze.

CONE TEMPERATURES

Cone temperatures are how we refer to the temperature a kiln is heated to. They are called cones because before digital kilns were made, kilns would be fired with pyrometric cones that measured heat-work, which is temperature and time to temperature. The most common cone temperatures include cones 05 and 06, which are considered low fire; cones 5 and 6, which are considered mid fire; and cone 10, which is high fire. Anything in between like a cone 7 or 8 is either advanced because you're formulating your own glaze, or it is a firing mistake and you will need to refire at the appropriate cone to allow your glaze to properly mature.

Knowing your cone temps is important because different clays and glazes require different temps. When you fire clay to its ideal temperature it vitrifies and turns its expected color. Most clays that are cone 5 and up will hold water. If you under-fire clay, it will not become vitrified nor will it hold water, and the color will be dull. Under-firing will also cause the clay to be porous, which is not good for food safety because food and bacteria can become trapped in the piece. Overfiring can cause melting. If you fire a mid-range clay or glaze in a high-temperature firing, you will end up with a puddle of clay or a pool of glaze that melted off your piece and onto the kiln shelf. Most likely, you will have to put a lot of work into the pricey kiln shelf if this mistake is made even if you use kiln wash. Kiln wash can only do so much and has limits. If there is too much glaze, even on kiln wash, it will damage the shelf. The pieces can also melt onto other pieces that are in the kiln and could possibly ruin someone else's work. It's crucial to pay attention to these details because if you are bringing pieces to a studio for firing, you don't want to break their equipment because you didn't check the temperature of your clay or glaze.

Remember, cone 05 and cone 5 are VERY different:

Cone 05/06—Low fire/bisque: This is generally used as a bisque firing, but it can be used for glaze as well.

Cone 5/6—Mid-range: This is the most common in electric kiln firings, very common for drinkware and dinnerware.

Cone 10: Common with gas firing and generally the most common highest temperature folks will go to.

CHECK YOUR LABELS

Every glaze you buy will have a cone range on the label. The label will also say if it's food safe certified, which is important if you are making anything you plan to eat or drink from. The

CONE	FAHRENHEIT	CENTIGRADE	
08	1.751	0.955	LOW-FIRE EARTHENWARE
07	1.803	0.984	
06	1.830	0.990	
05	1.914	1.046	
04	1.940	1.060	
03 ½	1.976	1.080	
03	2.014	1.101	
02	2.048	1.120	
01	2.079	1.137	
1	2.109	1.154	
2	2.124	1.162	
3	2.134	1.68	
4	2.167	1.186	MID-FIRE STONEWARE
5	2.165	1.196	
6	2.232	1.222	
7	2.264	1.240	
8	2.305	1.261	HIGH-FIRE
9	2.336	1.284	
10	2.381	1.305	
11	2.399	1.315	

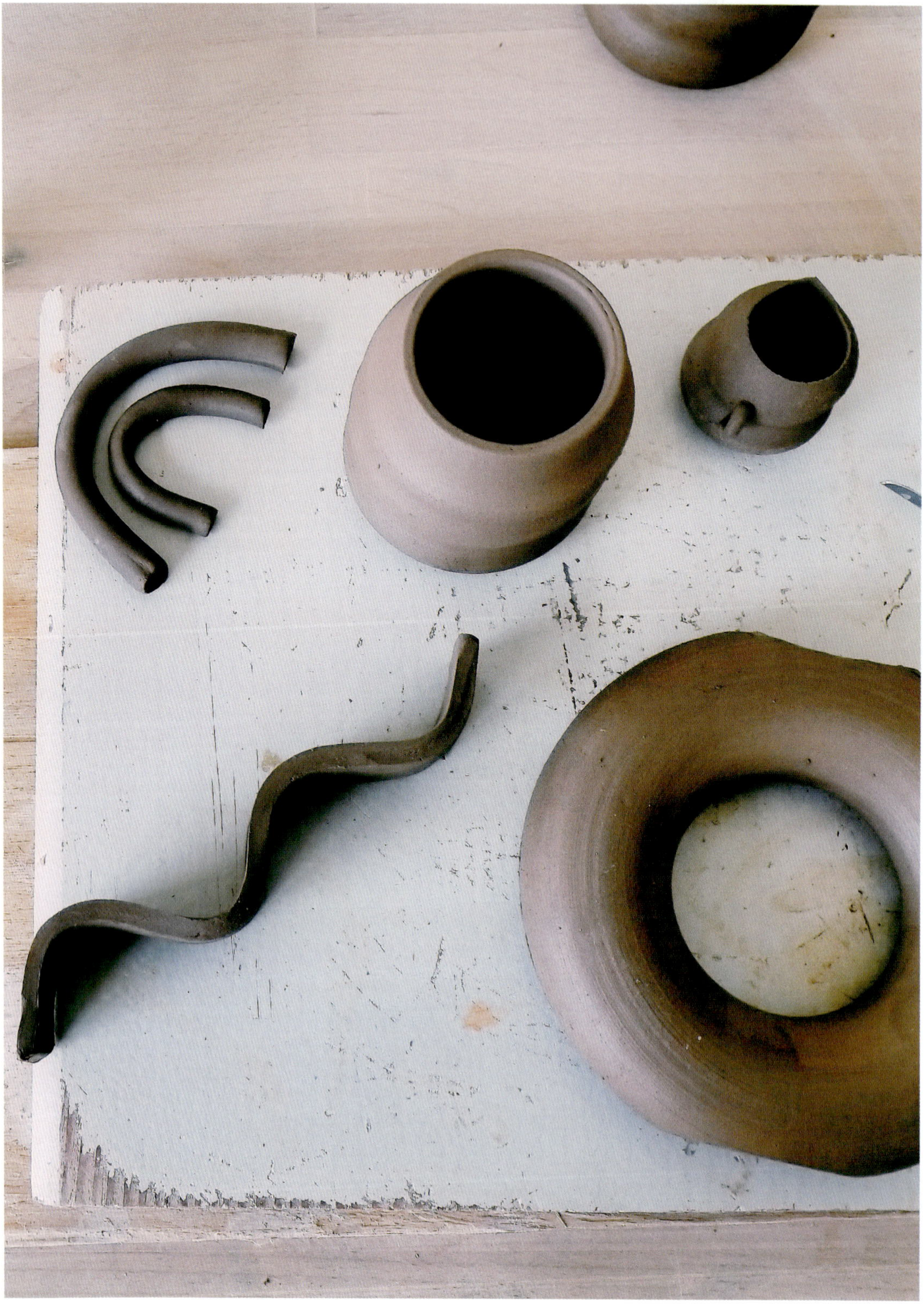

Safety Issues to Keep in Mind

Safety when working with ceramics is very important. Please read this section carefully before beginning any pottery projects.

Clay Dust: Clay contains silica, which if chronically inhaled can lead to lung cancer. It's important to mop often and keep your workspace as clean as possible. Remember, no sweeping. Sweeping causes dust to be kicked up into the air and into your lungs. Use a mop instead of a broom and when wiping surfaces, use a wet sponge or rag. If you ever need to sand, use the wet sanding method and do it outside.

Sharp Pieces: Whether scraping kiln shelves or handling a piece on which the glaze has bubbled, keep in mind how sharp glaze shards can be. Never graze your hand across a kiln shelf and be mindful of where you put your hands. Glaze drippings can be very sharp like glass and can cut you badly. If you are chipping glaze off kiln shelves, be sure to wear eye protection.

Glaze Dust: Glaze dust can be just as harmful as clay dust. If you spray on glaze, use lung protection, use proper ventilation, and keep your work area clean.

label should say it is non-toxic AND food-safe certified. Back in the day, glazes used to contain lead and all sorts of harmful ingredients but today most glazes are nontoxic. But remember, nontoxic does not necessarily mean food safe. Unless it specifically says "food safe certified" do not use it for food. On that note, if you ever find secondhand glazes at art supply reuse stores, be sure to keep safety in mind. I've found glazes on eBay and at secondhand art supply shops that were from the 1970s that had lead in them and should never have been resold.

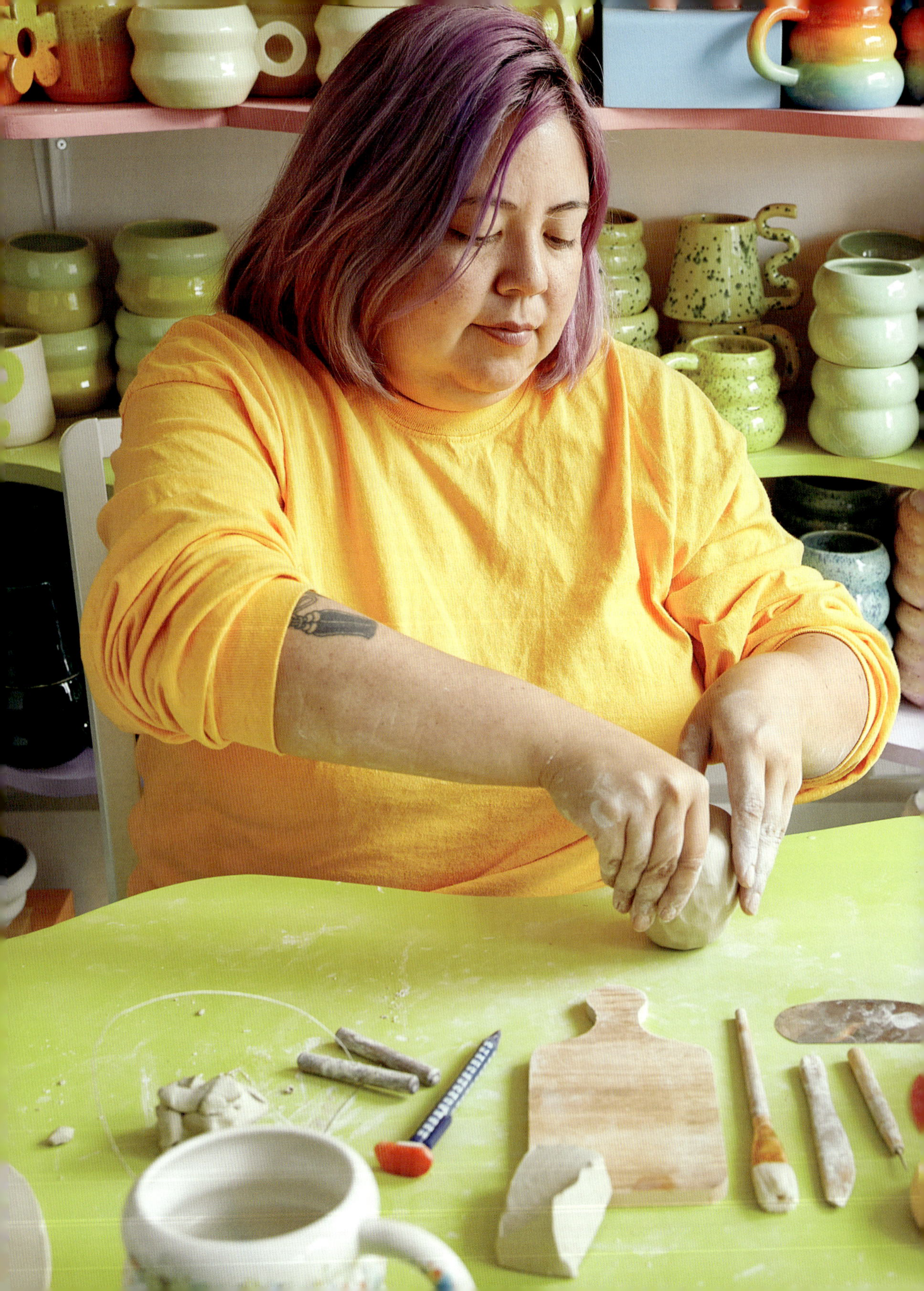

Pinch Pot Method

CHAPTER 2

Pinch Pot Method

Pinch pots are the most basic form of pottery. They go back to ancient times and the method is used to make simple cups and bowls. Pinch pots are very personal pieces of art because you can see the artist's hand in every step. You can see the artist's finger indentations and you can almost feel where their hands were when holding the piece.

Key Term

Score and slip: How you attach pieces together in pottery. Make hash marks with your needle tools on each side of where the clay will meet. Add slip and press the pieces together firmly. Smooth out the seams.

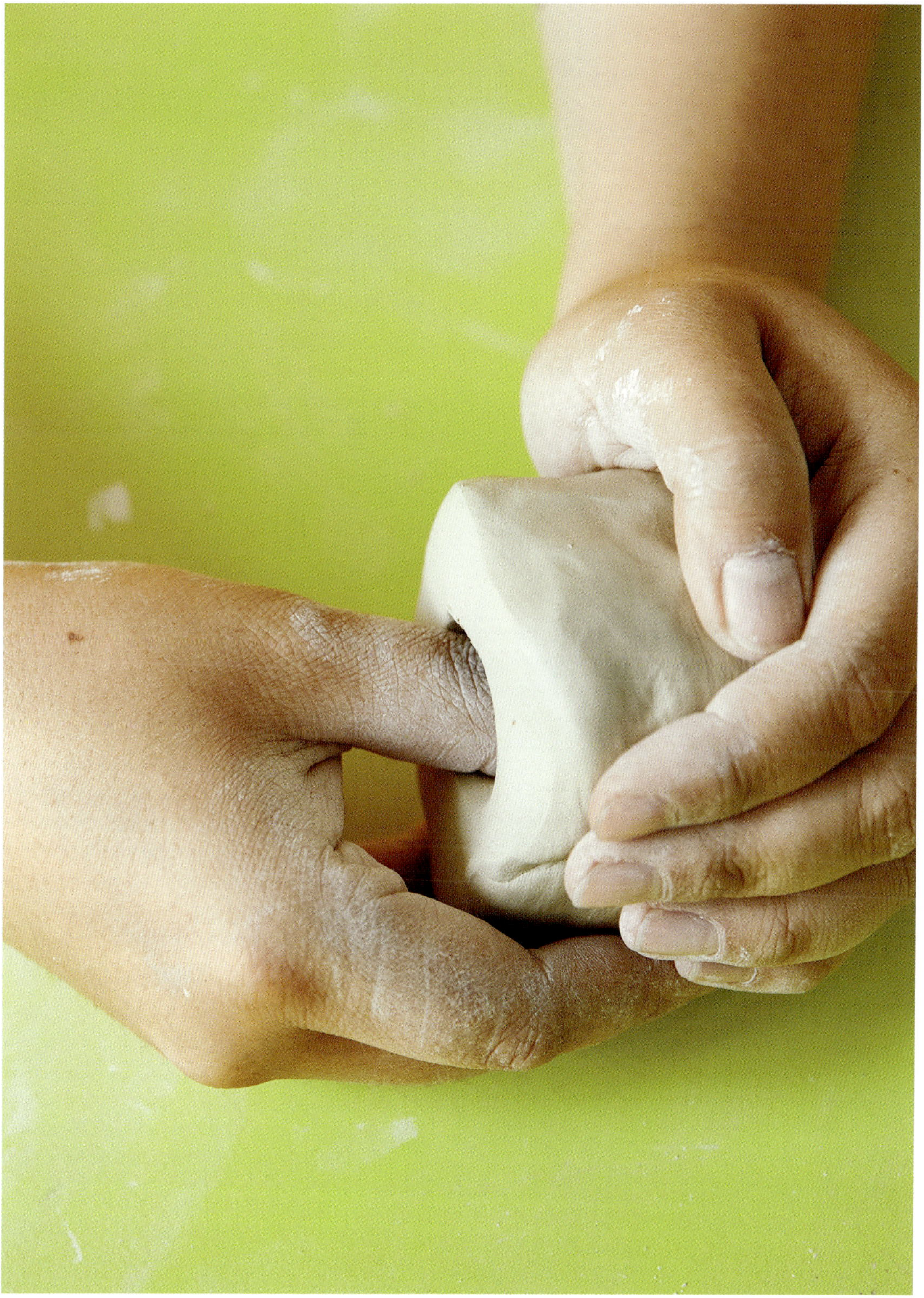

How to Make a Pinch Pot

Making a pinch pot is a perfect project for a beginner. Follow the steps below to create your first masterpiece.

TOOLS

CLAY
CUTTING WIRE
BOWL OF WATER
NEEDLE TOOL
SPONGE
CLAY KNIFE
POROUS SURFACE

1 Prepare your surface: The surface you are working on needs to be porous. An unfinished wood surface or a wood slab covered in canvas is ideal.

2 Get your area ready: Clay is messy. You don't want to be running all over your house with drippy clay-covered hands looking for your sponge.

3 Get a manageable amount of clay. If you are making a small cup, an apple-sized clay piece would be good **A**.If you're making a bowl, a grapefruit-sized ball would be best.

4 Once you decide on the amount of clay you need, use a cutting wire to cut it off the block **B**. Cutting wires are just like cheese wires and they slice through the clay easily **C**. If you don't have a cutting wire, a long piece of floss will do. Once you cut your cube, shape it into a ball, which sounds simple; however, this requires special care when making ceramics. You will need to be mindful of air bubbles.

5 Form the clay into a ball by patting the corners of the sides while making sure you aren't tapping any air inside. An area that seems like it is a fold reminds me of waves at the beach. You don't want to make those types of waves with barrels that you see surfers going through because that just creates a big air hole. You want to be the wave that pushes out but never folds over.

6 Once the clay is in a ball, hold it in your non-dominant hand, cup it firmly, and then press in with the thumb from your other hand **D**. Don't go all the way to the bottom. You will have to estimate the thickness of the bottom but start off thick because it is easier to trim off clay than it is to add on more. The pressure you want to put on the clay is similar to a light massage. Keep cupping the clay securely in your non-dominant hand. If your hand flattens or you cup it too loosely, you will end up with more of a plate than a cup. The hand holds the structure of the clay and sets a precedent for the shape.

7 Pinch the clay upward while rotating the piece to get an even shape **E**. Keep the rim on the thicker side. When folks first start learning this method, they tend to make the rims too thin, which leads to cracking and limits how the piece can be used. Eventually, you will see your cup begin to form.

Violà! You have a pinch pot **F** ! Now you can try this method with a bigger piece of clay and make a bowl or try making a double pinch pot!

Note: With pinch pots it's best to make the surface as smooth as possible—especially nail marks that can become sharp after firing.

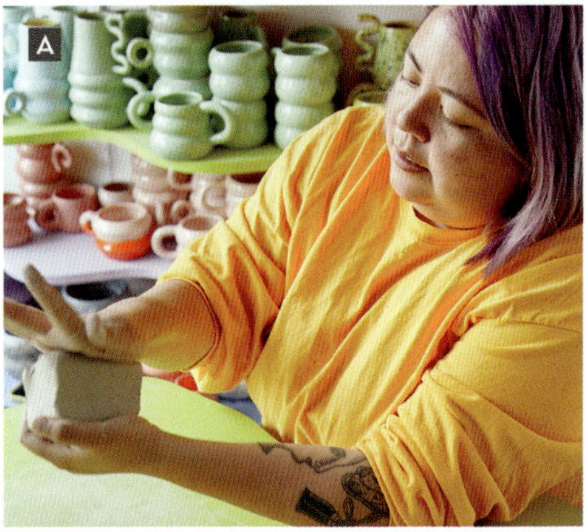
A

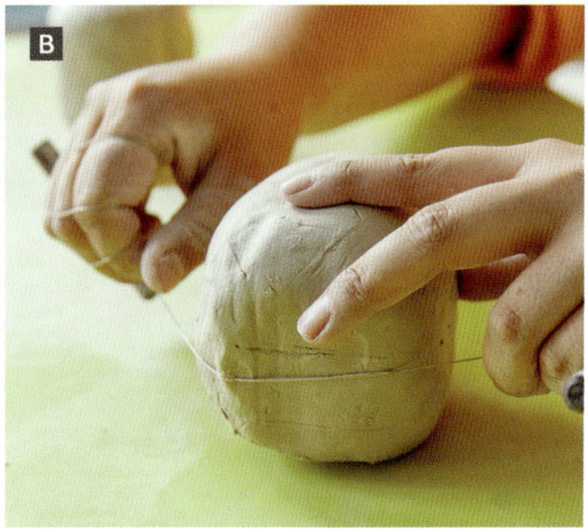
B

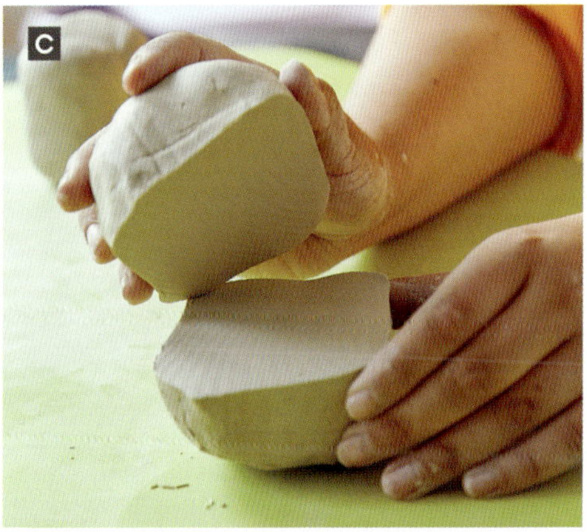
C

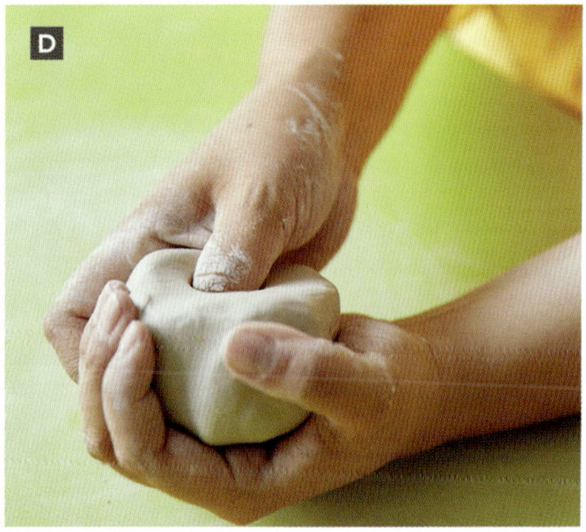
D

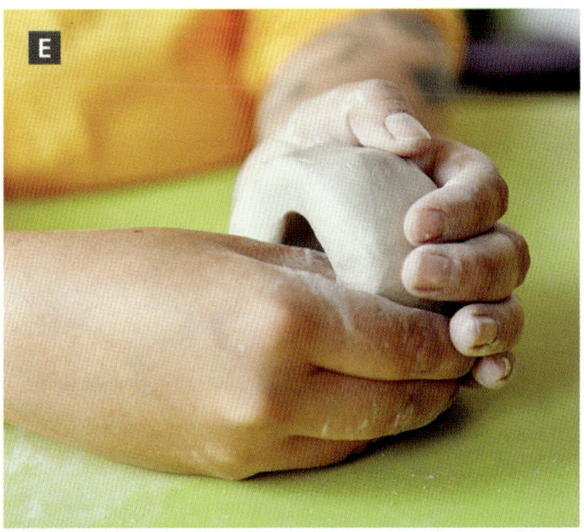
E

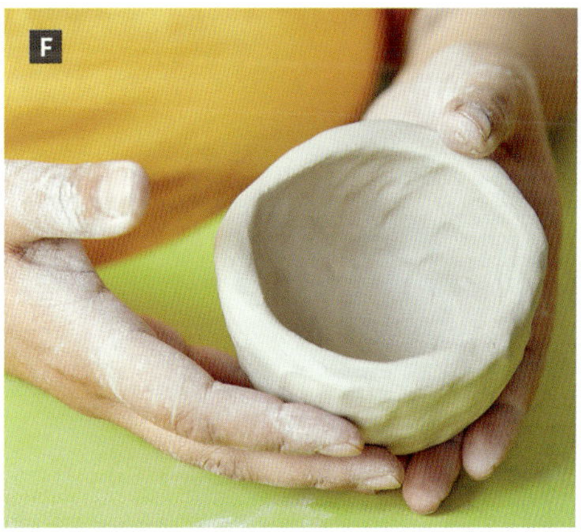
F

How to Make a Double Pinch Pot

Double pinch pots are when you make two pots of similar size and then score and slip them together to make a hollow ball. "Score and slip" is how you make sure anything in clay holds together (see below for more details). What's so special about a hollow ball? When you make this hollow ball you have trapped air inside, which you can actually use to your advantage as the air pressure inside the ball can help keep your piece from collapsing while you are working on it. You could gently roll your double pinch pot out to a more oblong shape or a flat-topped shape all while the air stabilizes your piece.

Eventually, you'll need to make a small hole to let the air out. Don't forget this step! If you don't allow the air to escape, your piece will explode in the kiln, and if you wait until the piece is dry to the point where the shrinking has started, then the pressure from the air inside can distort the piece at weak points or crack it before it even gets the chance to be fired.

Follow these steps to make a double pinch pot:

1. Make a ball of clay and cut it in half as equally as possible.
2. Follow the steps from the How to Make a Pinch Pot section above to make two pinch pots and make the rims of both as close to the same diameter as possible **A**. Kiss the rims together to see if you need to rework any sides.
3. Flatten out the rims by lightly tapping them flat against the surface you're working on.
4. Score the tops of the rims with a needle tool **B**.
5. Add water or slip (watered down clay) to the rims.
6. Attach the rims together by cupping both pinch pots and then apply pressure when the rims meet **C**. This pressure needs to be evenly distributed. I like to say it's the kind of pressure you put on an avocado to see if it is ripe. You don't just stab the avocado with your fingers to see if its ripe, you cup it and apply even pressure.
7. Once the two pots are secured together you can smooth out the seam **D**. Remember the ocean waves metaphor: You are not making a wave with a barrel that a little surfer can go through, you are making a little kiddie wave that never folds over. You can do a final smoothing with a wet sponge **E**.
8. Once everything is connected you can start playing with the trapped air **F**. You could roll the piece gently with your hands to make a burrito form and cut a hole at the top to make a vase or a taller tumbler.

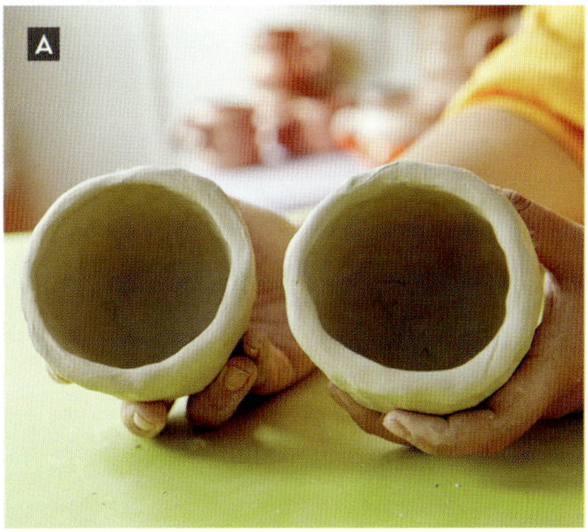
A

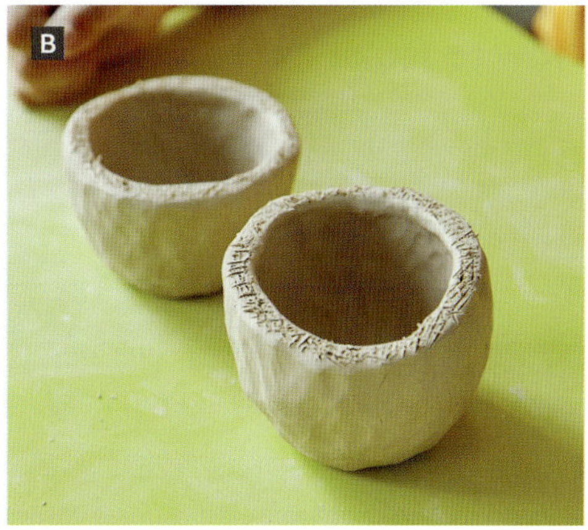
B

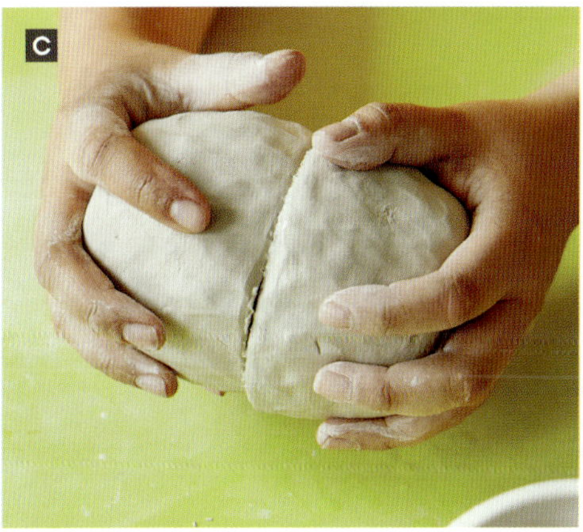
C

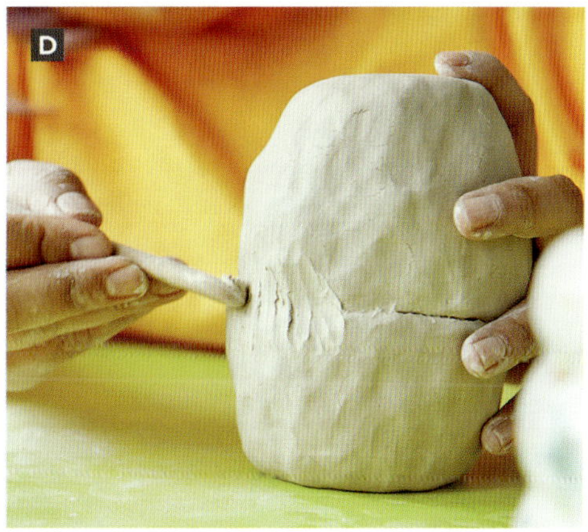
D

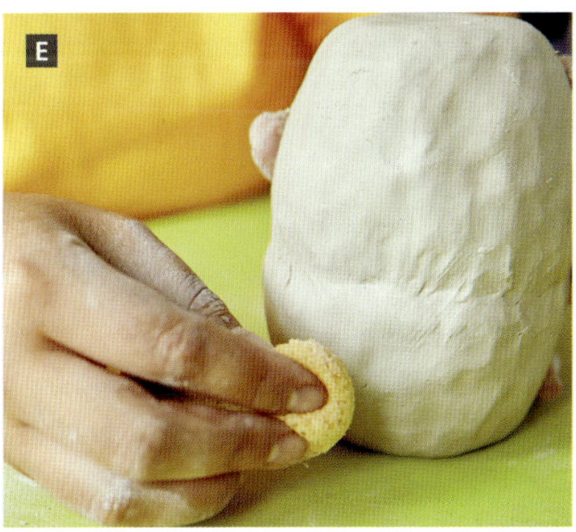
E

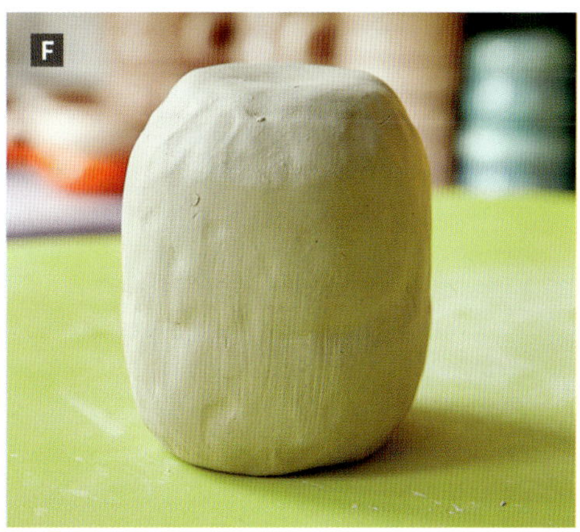
F

How to Make Attachments

To add attachments like handles, knobs, or decorative bits, you'll need to score and slip as follows:

1. Roll out your handles **A**.
2. Wherever you want to add an attachment, make hatch marks with your needle tool **B**. Attach the first slip **C**.
3. Make hatch marks with your needle tool on both pieces of an attachment and then apply the other slip **D**.
4. Once the slip has been applied **E**, then smooth out the meeting points for a stronger hold.
5. Attach the two pieces **F**, and apply pressure.

Air Bubbles and Explosions

Air bubbles trap moisture in clay. When a piece that is seemingly dry has air bubbles and is fired, the air and moisture become trapped in little pockets. When the temperature goes up and the clay starts to contract, the moisture turns to steam and needs to go somewhere, so it bursts out of the clay causing an explosion.

Explosions happen often in ceramics, it's just the name of the game. Explosions can happen from air pockets or moisture that is still in the clay when firing. Sometimes explosions can happen due to the type of clay being used. Some clays are fickle and don't like certain types of firings, though these occurrences are rare. Explosions aren't fun for multiple reasons. Of course, your piece will be ruined if it explodes, but an explosion can also ruin the piece next to it inside the kiln. Furthermore, if something with glaze on it explodes, the glaze becomes like sharp shards of glass and will stick to other pieces, the kiln shelf, and the inner walls of the kiln. This means many hours of extra work.

How to prevent explosions, you ask? Make sure the clay is properly wedged to get all the air out before forming your piece. Also make sure your pieces are absolutely bone dry before firing. Set your kiln to go at a slow setting. This will give excess moisture time to steam out. I will sometimes leave the top peephole open on my kiln to make sure the steam from excess moisture has somewhere to go. Steam can also affect the glazes, causing bubbling, so keep that in mind if you are doing a bisque and a glaze firing at the same time. You can do many different types of slow firing methods and you could also candle the kiln. Candling is when you hold the kiln to just 200 degrees Fahrenheit for a long period of time (six hours average). This turns up the heat just enough to allow moisture to escape without going too high and helps to keep your pieces from exploding. Explosions usually happen around 400 degrees Fahrenheit. Candling is used a lot for sculptural pieces and large pieces because those types of work have the tendency to trap moisture in little pockets more than others.

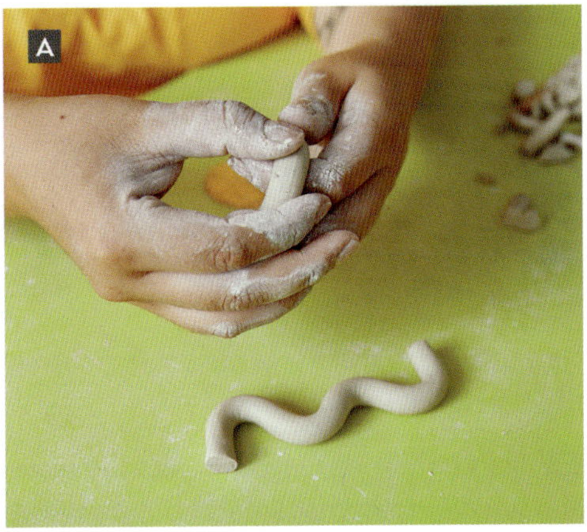
A

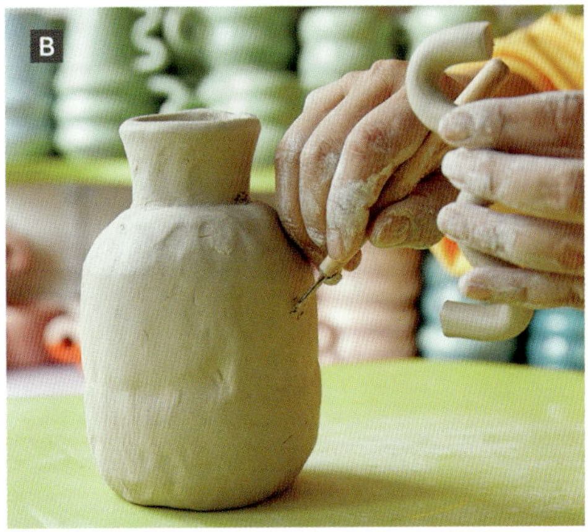
B

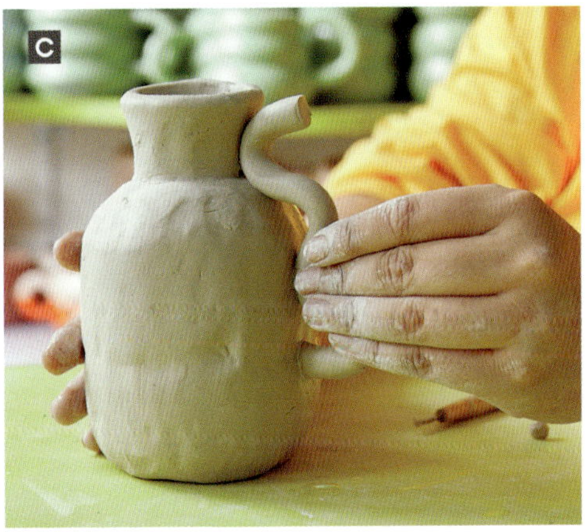
C

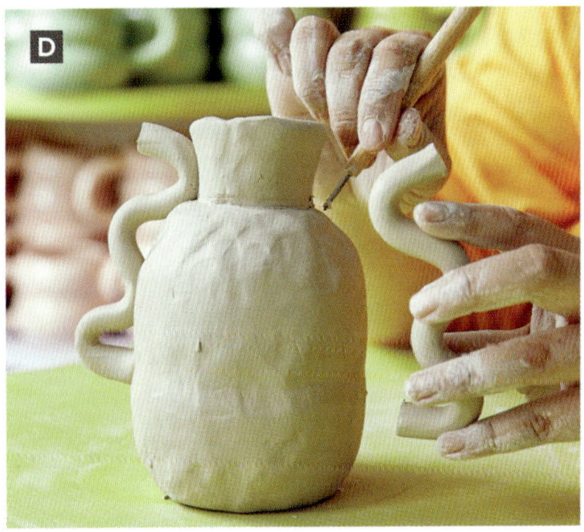
D

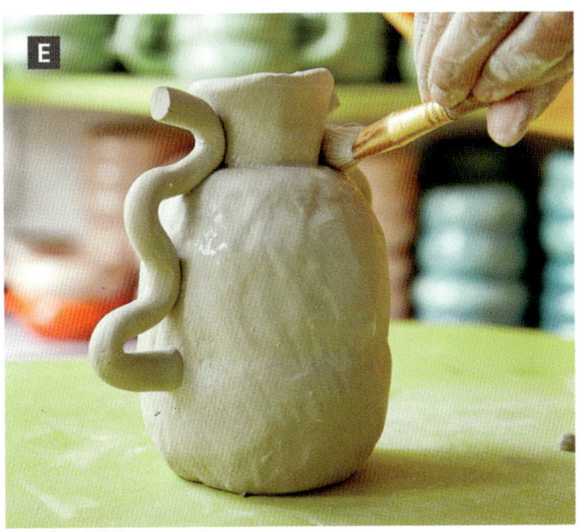
E

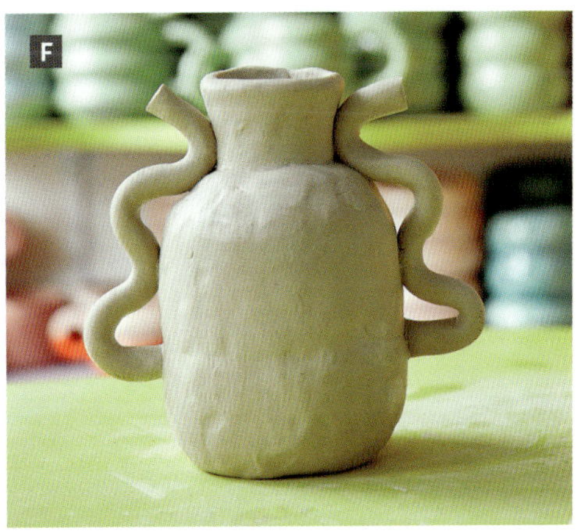
F

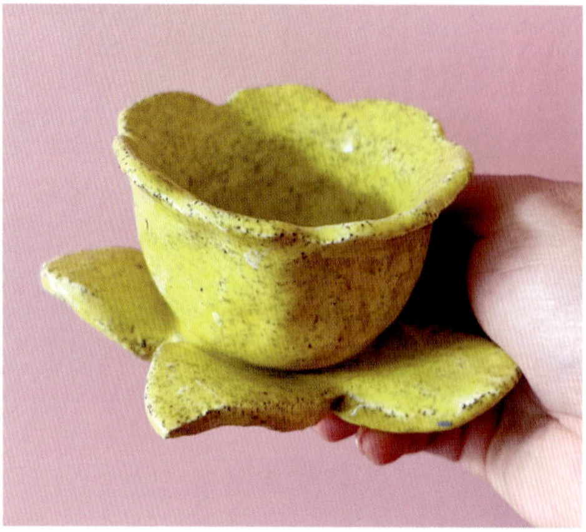

Pinch Pot Picnic Inspiration

Pinch pots have so much character and can be very expressive. This project is a great beginner project. This is also a way to troubleshoot practicality of ideas.

First, draw out some things that remind you of a picnic—flowers, watermelons, food, and more. Draw out how you will turn these pieces into usable tableware. Add handles, saucers, and functional elements. This is where you need to picture the functionality of your piece. For example, if you're making a pinch pot mug the shape of a strawberry, consider the shape of the top of the strawberry. The shoulders arch in so you must imagine how that would feel to drink out of. Maybe that shape would make a better vase or a plate? How about handles? Is it taller than the mug? That might hit your face when you drink out of it. What if you were making a picnic basket mug? The flat edges might make your drink go everywhere so maybe that shape would be better as a bowl. Play with scale. How about a jumbo pear cookie jar? Assess which method would be best to make each piece. Slabs for plates? Pinch for bowls?

Now it's time to make your pieces! I'm making this dandelion sugar bowl.

1. Start by making two pinch pots and score and slip them together. Smooth out the seam.
2. You can use the air trapped inside to help you form your piece. Roll out your shape and, when you are satisfied, make sure you make an air hole for firing so it doesn't explode.
3. Start adding decorative pieces like outside petals.
4. When your piece has firmed up a bit you can start moving the petals to make them look more organic.
5. With a moist sponge, smooth out the inside seam where the pinch pots meet and the outer edges.
6. Set to bisque fire, glaze, and fire again. Then you're done!

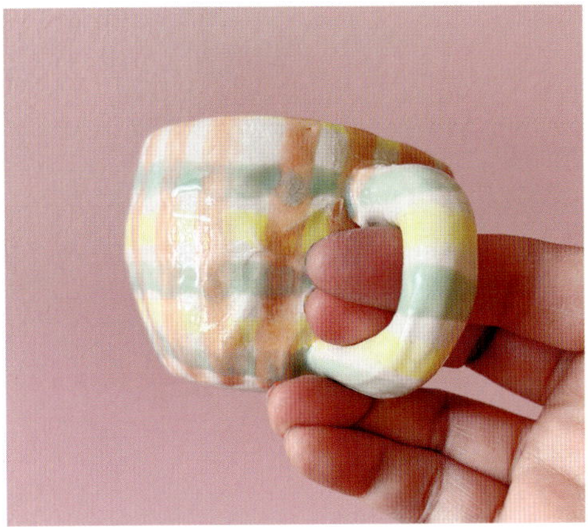
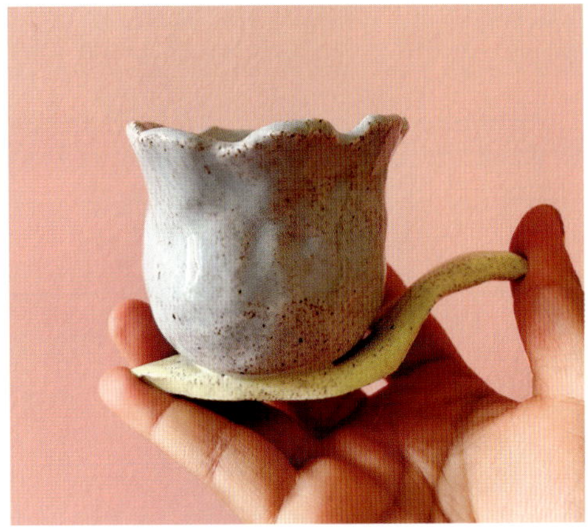
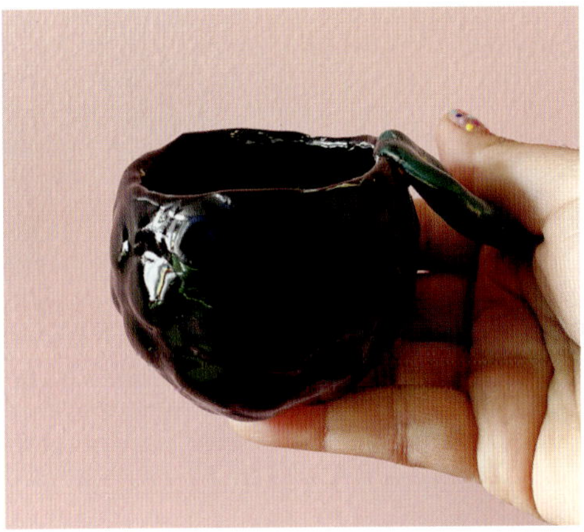
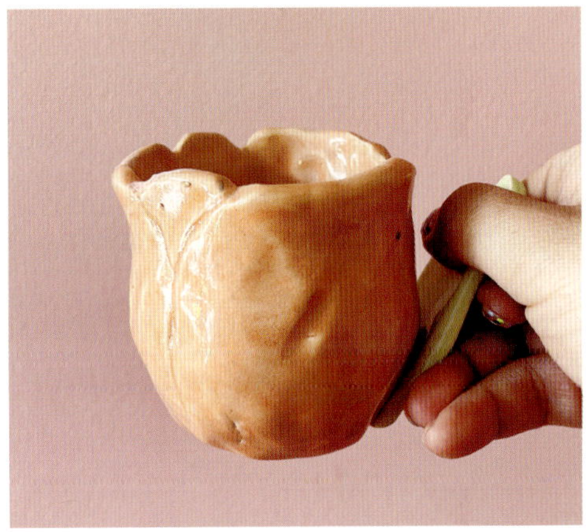
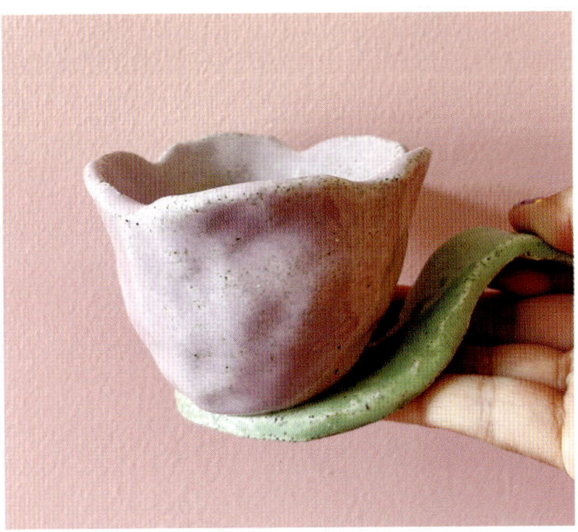
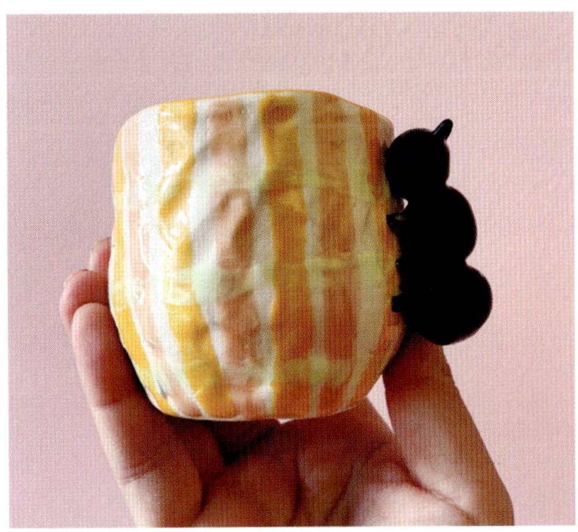

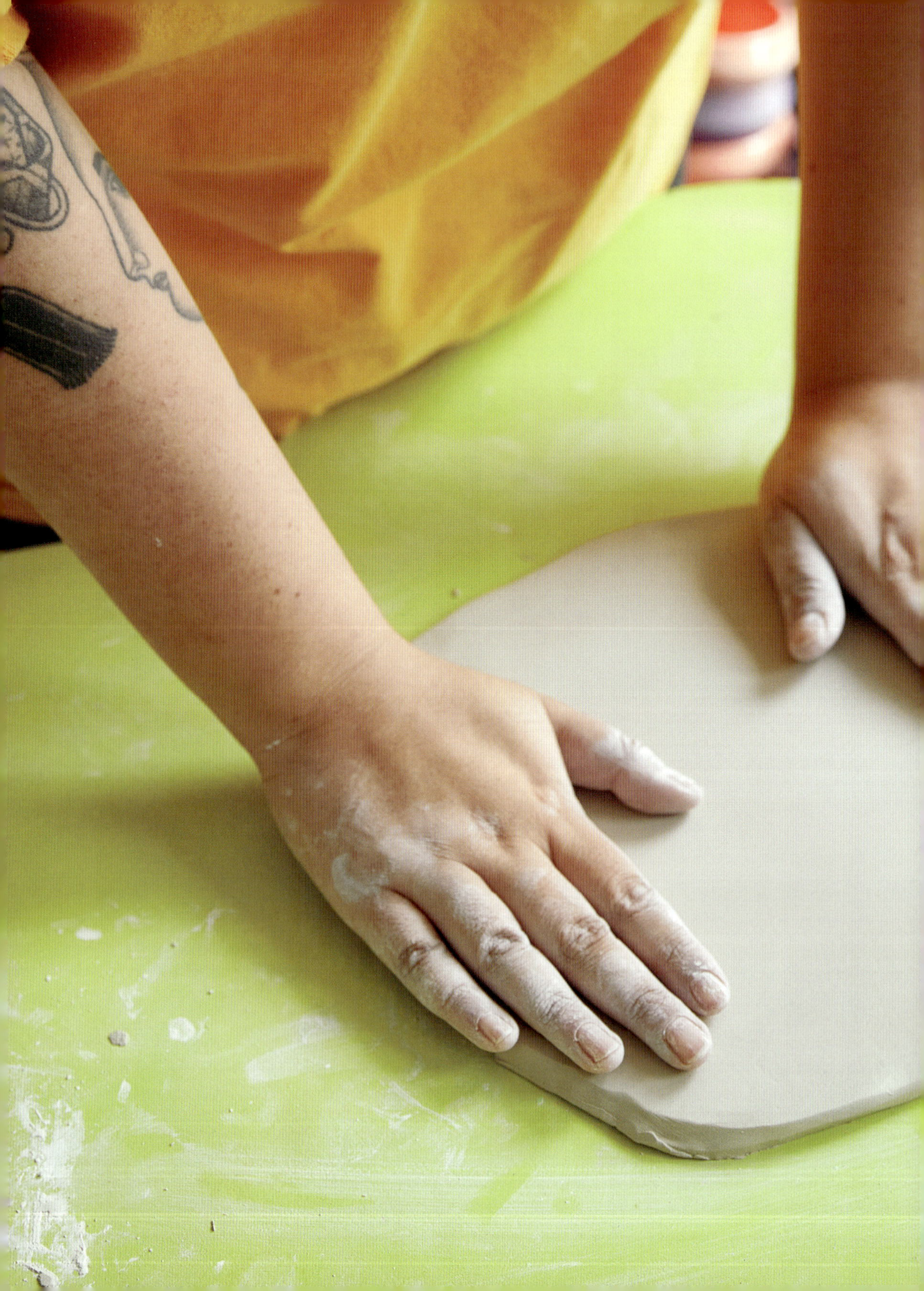

Slab Building

CHAPTER 3

Slab Building

Slab building is a method of ceramics where you roll out clay to form flat sheets and let them dry to be as hard as leather. This state will make the clay rigid enough to build geometric pieces. If you are making a box of any kind, slab building is the best method to use. Slab building can be so fun. You can play with the drapability of the clay, and you can use items from around the house as forms. You can drape thin slabs of clay, like thick fabric, in or over a form and the clay will take on its shape.

Key Terms

Hump form: A convex form you drape a clay slab over. The interior surface of your piece is in contact with the mold. This is one of two basic types of molds used when slab building.

Slump form: A concave form you drape a clay slab into. The inside surface of your piece is exposed while the outer face is in contact with the mold. Along with hump form, this is one of two basic types of molds used when slab building.

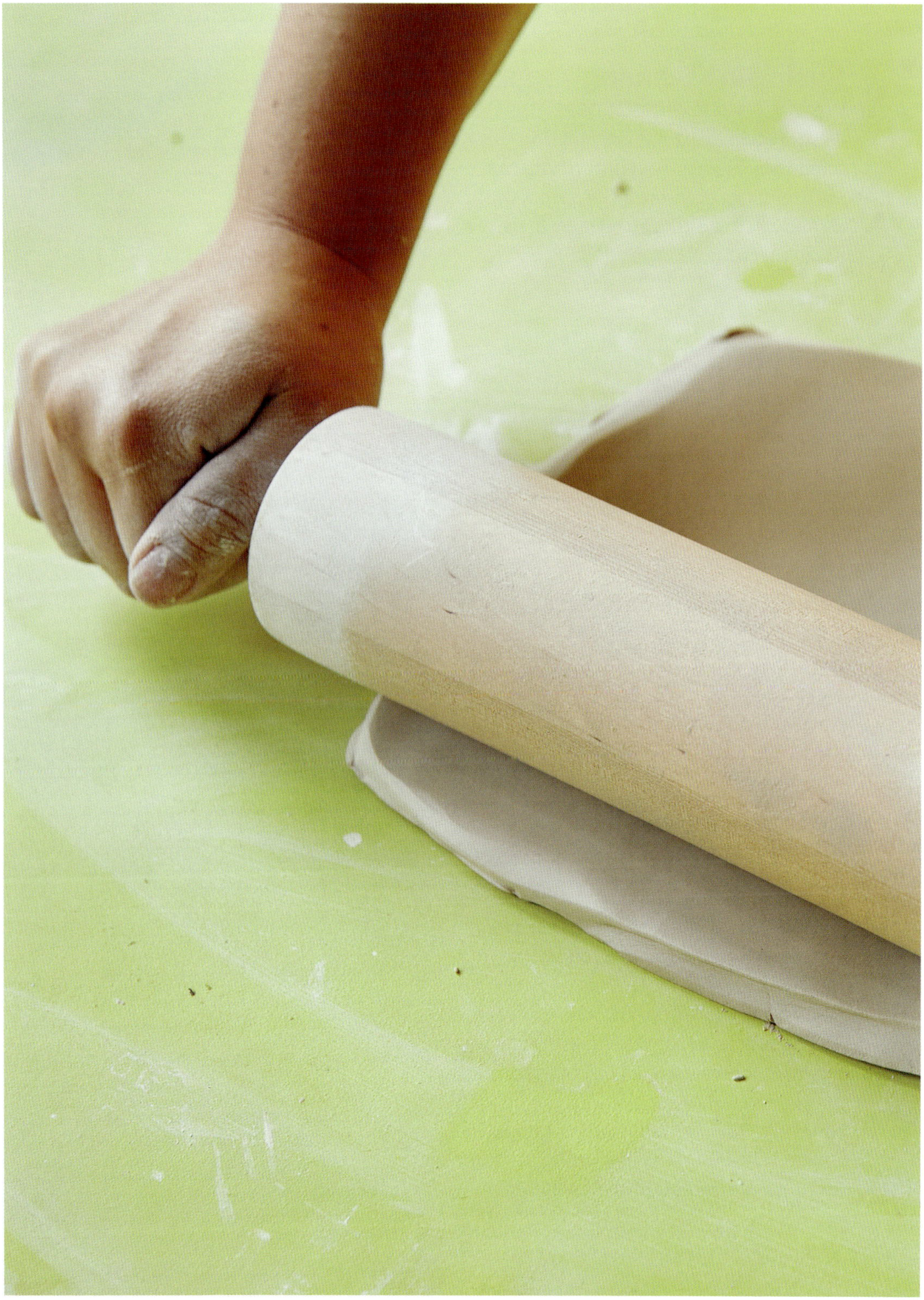

Basic Slab Building

Prepare your project. If you are making something geometric, it is a good idea to use a template to ensure all the pieces will fit correctly. You can use slab building to make a box or a rectangular vase.

TOOLS

CLAY
ROLLING PIN
METAL RIB
NEEDLE TOOL
SPONGE
CUTTING WIRE
MULTIPLE WOODEN BOARDS
SHEETS OF CANVAS
CLAY KNIFE

EXTRA SLAB BUILDING TOOLS

You can use wooden guides to make sure your slabs are equal in thickness. I use long paint stir sticks. Put them on each side of the clay piece within the width of the rolling pin and then roll out the slab. You can also use a slab roller if you have access to one.

Follow these steps to make your first slab-building project:

1. Cut off a couple pieces of clay with your wire tool **A** and roll them out on a porous surface with a wooden rolling pin. Be careful when you move your rolled-out pieces because, remember, clay has memory. Keep each slab as flat as possible while transferring them to boards and try not to drape the slabs.

Note: Slab building is all about the timing. The clay needs to be just firm enough to stay stiff for building but still moist enough to score, slip, and attach. The slabs all need to dry at the same rate so try to keep their environment the same. For example, if you are drying your slabs in a room, be sure to keep them away from the window. Uneven dryness can cause cracking and torquing. You can cut a small sample piece from the side of the slab to see if it has reached the desired firmness. It should be as firm as a freshly baked cookie and the surface should look like leather with a bit of sheen. The clay should not appear matte at all. If it does, that means it has dried too long.

2. Once all the slabs are at the desired dryness, you can use your clay knife to cut out the pieces from the template **B**. Cut all the pieces in one sitting. It's best to use slip rather than water for attachments for slabs.

3. Score and slip all edges that will touch and then start attaching **C**. Firmly press the pieces together without distorting the shape. Smooth out the seams using a brush or a sponge **D**. Attaching all these pieces at once can feel like juggling, so make sure you have heavy items on hand to hold the walls in place while you are working **E** **F**.

4. Drape plastic loosely over the piece so that it can dry slowly to avoid cracking.

Note: Make sure you put something porous between the clay and the form so you'll be able to remove the piece (unless you are using a plaster form). Don't leave the piece to dry in a form because the clay will hold water causing the piece to dry unevenly, which can cause warping. Also, if you're using a hump form and you leave your piece on it too long, it will shrink around the form and lead to cracking.

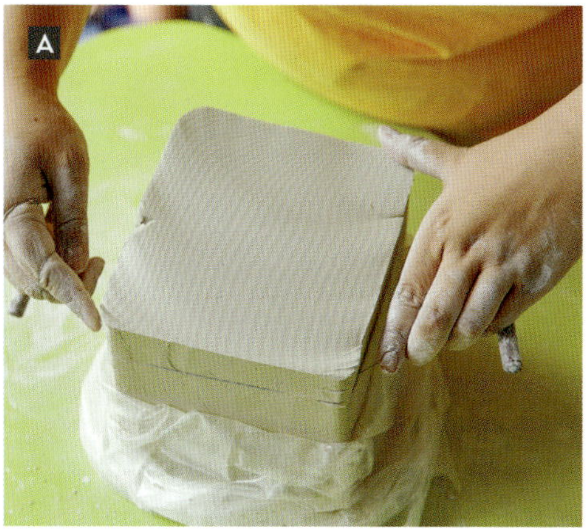
A

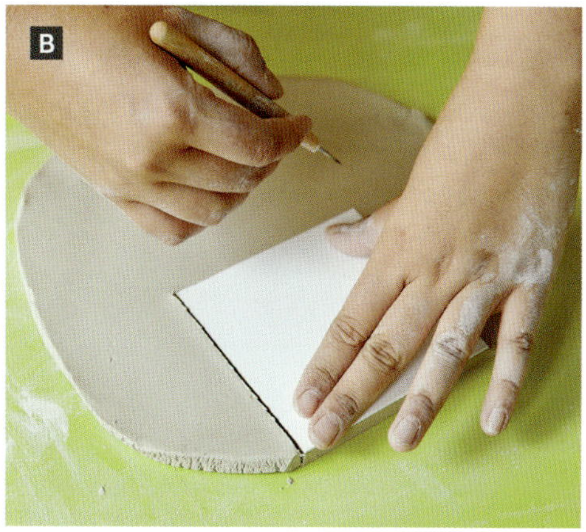
B

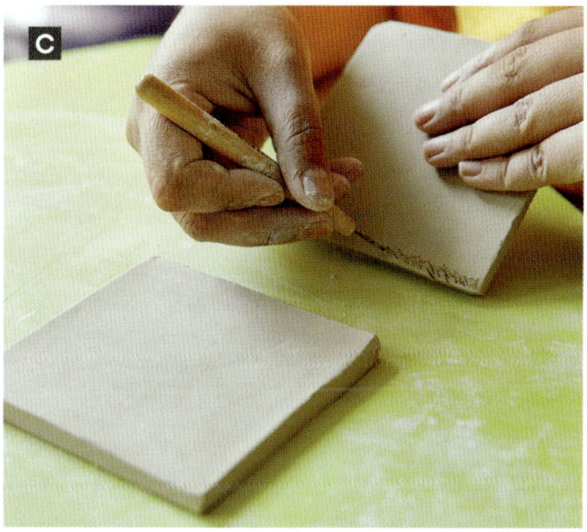
C

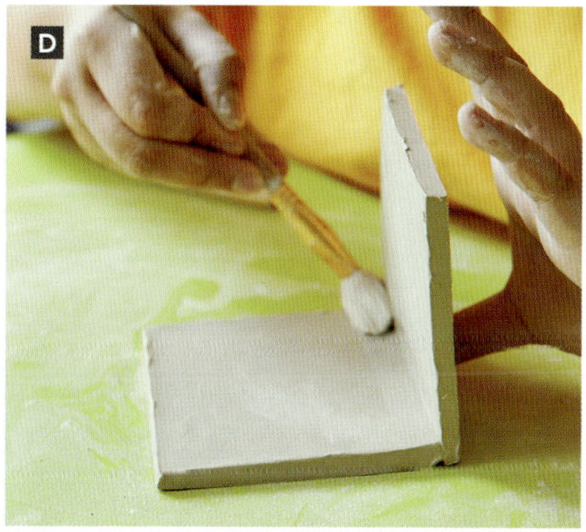
D

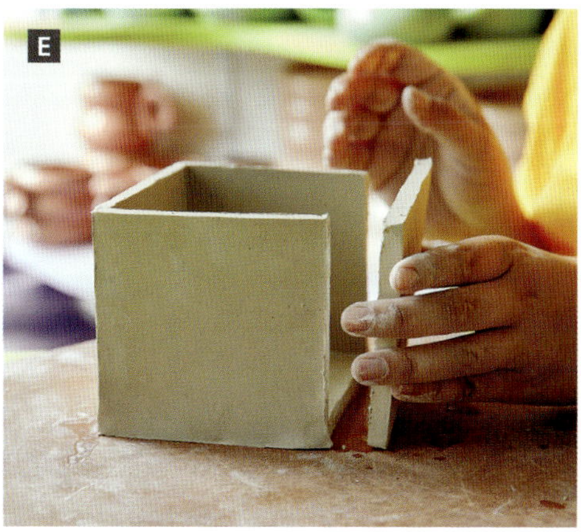
E

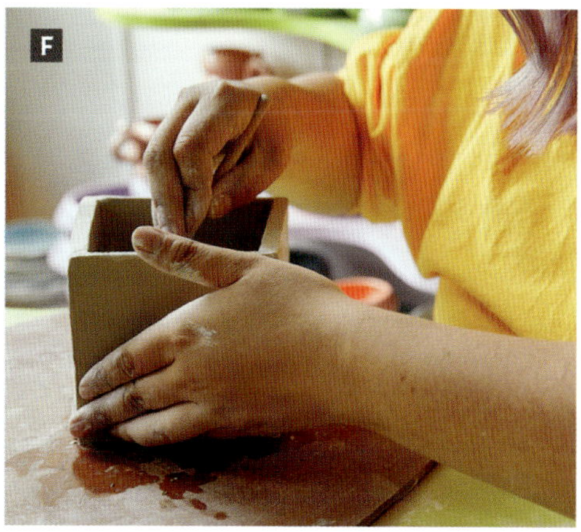
F

Making a Rounded Vase

To make a rounded vase while using the slab-building method, follow these steps:

1. Roll out a slab and let it dry to almost leather hard so it's still flexible enough to be draped.
2. Grab a tube of some sort. You can make one out of scrap cardboard. Wrap the tube in one or two sheets of newspaper. Tape the paper to itself, not to the form.
3. Trim the bottom of your slab with a straight edge. A ruler can work great for this purpose. Trim the sides of the slabs making sure the corners are at 90 degrees. This will make your life easier to make the bottom even.
4. Wrap the slab around the newspaper-wrapped cardboard form and cut a line straight down where the clay wraps over itself and remove the excess. Score and slip the seam and then smooth it out.
5. Pull out the cardboard form first and then peel out the newsprint. Smooth out the inside of the seam. Now you have a clay tube!
6. Stand the clay tube on another smaller slab and trace the base of the vase. Cut out the base of the vase.
7. Score, slip, and attach the base. Smooth out the seams.

Violà! You've got a vase! You also have learned the skills needed to make a tumbler, mug, dish, or whatever you want using this method.

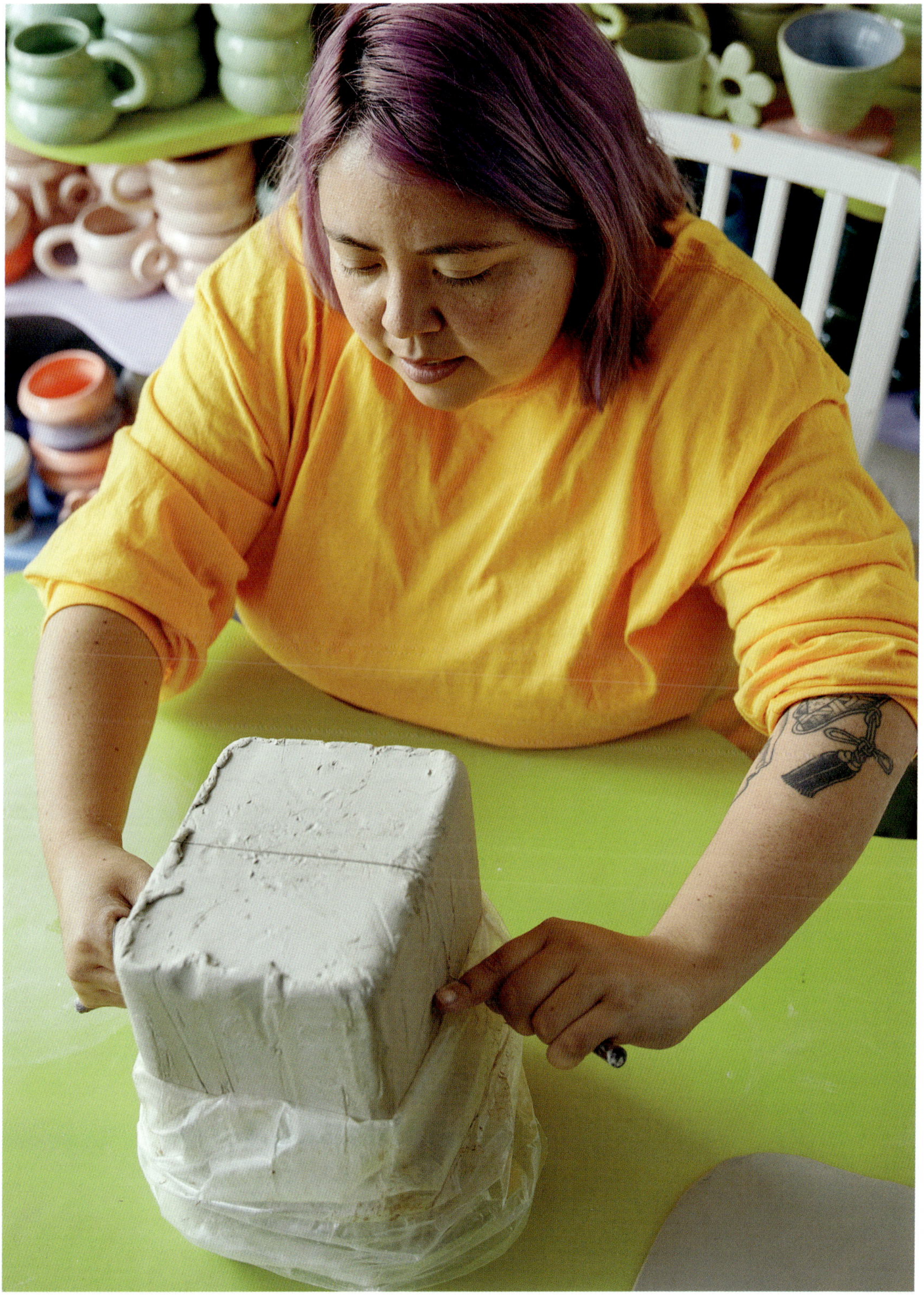

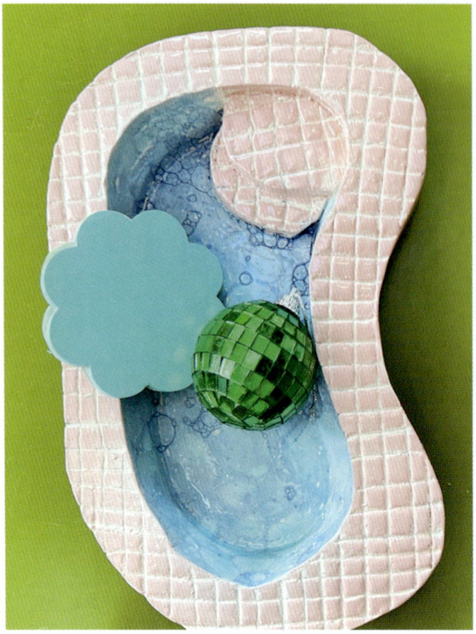

Bubble Glaze Swimming Pool Catch All

Put your new slab-building and bubble-glazing skills to use with this cute mini swimming pool!

TOOLS

CLAY
ROLLING PIN
NEEDLE TOOL
LONG RULER
SLIP
WOODEN BOARDS

1 Roll out two slabs to desired length and width and make sure they're at least ½ inch thick **A**. Don't forget to prevent warping—don't bend or drape the slab.

2 Cut your pool shape out of paper **B**. This could be classic oval, round, or kidney shaped. Don't go too intricate or have any sharp angles.

3 On one slab, cut out your pool shape from your template. On the second slab, cut out your pool top, which will be about 1 ½ inches from your template edges. Put aside to firm up. Put a sheet of cling wrap over the slab.

4 Grab your first slab and your ruler and press over the cling wrap to make a grid. Don't press all the way through! Just enough to make an impression **C**. This is how you'll make the appearance of tiles. The cling wrap will make the "tiles" look rounded which will look more realistic.

5 Peel back the cling wrap and set the slab to firm up to a leather-hard stage.

6 Cut out your pool top, which will be about 1 ½ inches from your template edges **D**. Put aside to firm up.

7 Roll a long slab the length of the perimeter of your pool base. It doesn't have to be exact but longer is preferred.

8 Cut a long strip from the slab about 2 ½ inches wide for the walls of the pool.

9 Cover the long slab with a sheet of cling wrap and make grid impressions with a ruler but leave ½ inch on one side of the width so we can attach it to the pool slab.

10 Score the ½ inch of slab. Grab your pool slab and score the edges.

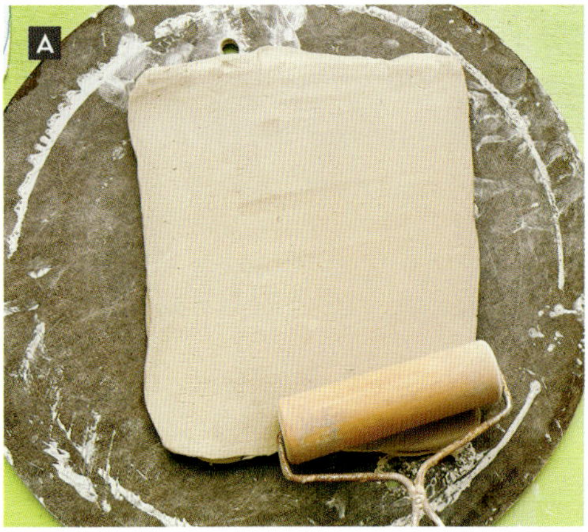
A

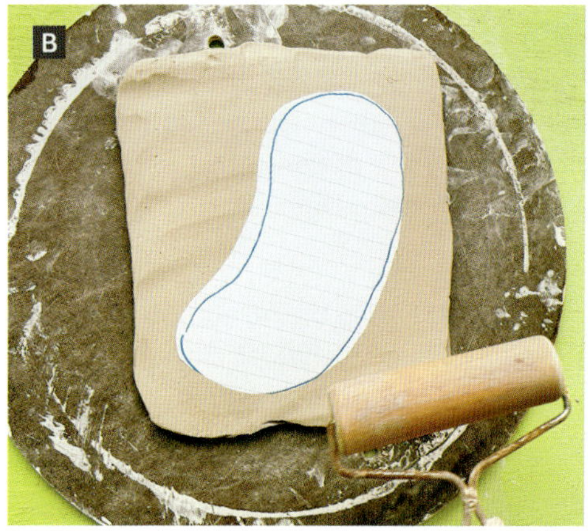
B

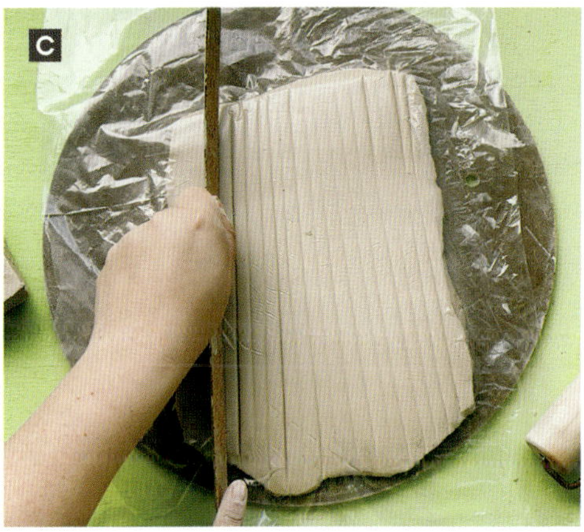
C

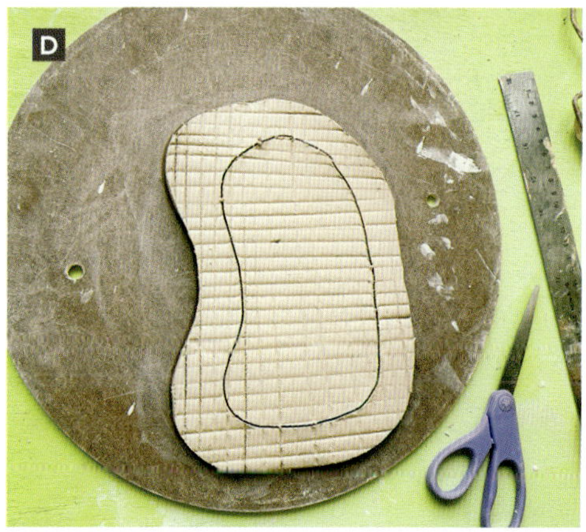
D

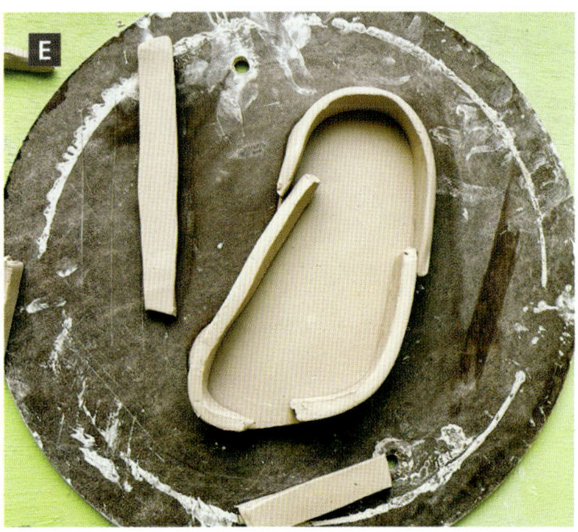
E

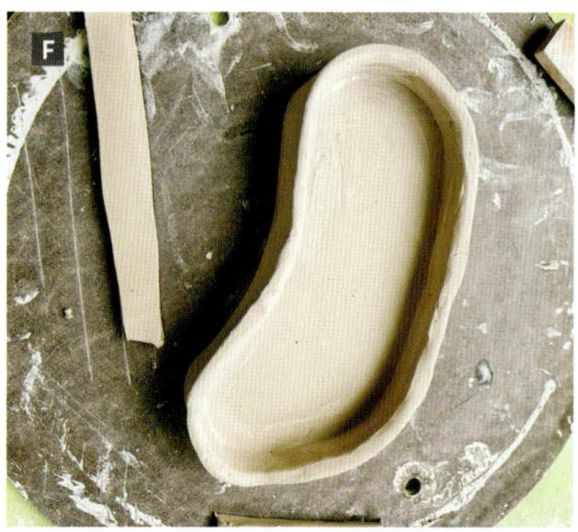
F

11 Pull the long slab (pool wall slab) along the rim of the pool base (you are not attaching yet). Your long slab should overlap and cut down the middle of where they both meet **E**. Dispose of the extra bits.

12 Grab some slip and slip both pieces that are scored as well as the meeting points for the pool walls. Press the wall pieces to the pool base and press the meeting place for the walls together.

13 Smooth out the meeting points. You can use a brush to smooth the meeting points or your finger **F**.

14 Set the pool aside until the pool has firmed up enough for the walls to not move when you touch it but soft enough to still work with.

15 Grab the pool top. It should be firm. Score and slip the attachment and smooth out attachment points **G**.

16 Take a board and place it on top of the pool. Flip the piece over using the boards. Smooth out the bottom of the pool.

17 Tent the piece to allow the piece to dry slowly. Once the piece is bone dry, set it to bisque.

18 Once dry, glaze the tiles to your desired pattern **H**. Brush wax resist delicately to the top of the pool so the bubble glaze doesn't affect the top.

19 It's bubble glaze time! Mix a light-blue underglaze: 3 drops of dish soap, one tablespoon of underglaze. Add 5 oz of water **I**. Mix together.

20 Grab a straw and a deep bowl and add the mix. Blow bubbles through the straw and allow the bubbles to overflow into the pool **J**. Make sure it's just the bubbles and don't pour the bubble mix straight into the pool. Let the bubbles pop on their own.

21 Wipe any extra underglaze off the wax resist. Set to fire. You're done! You should have a super-cute pool **K**.

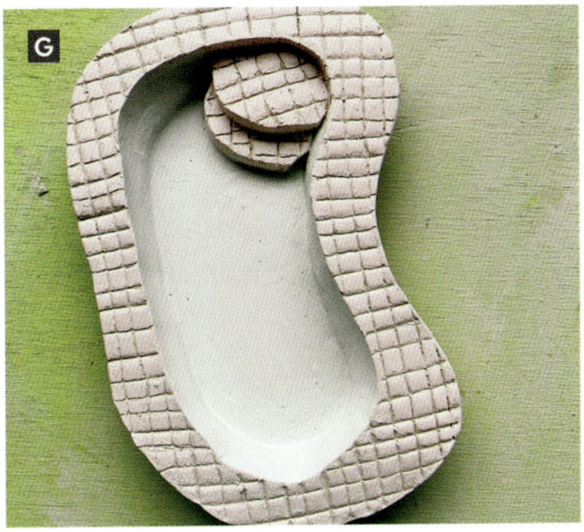
G

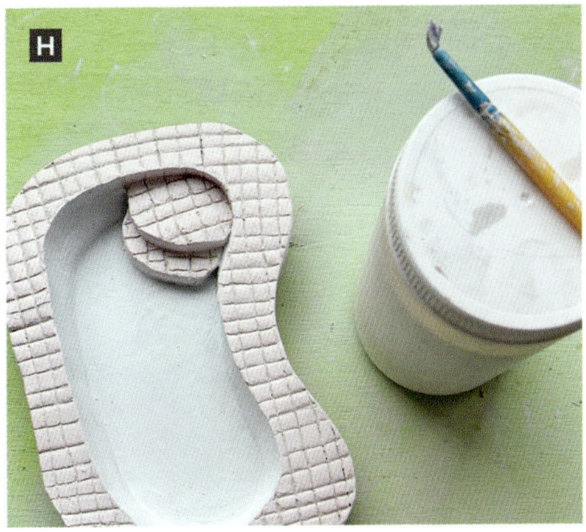
H

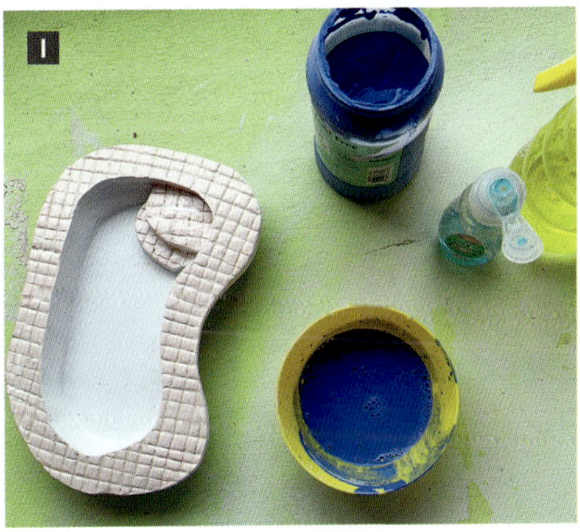
I

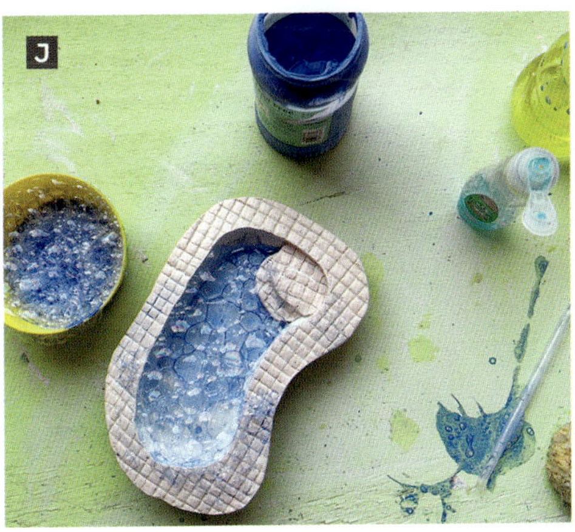
J

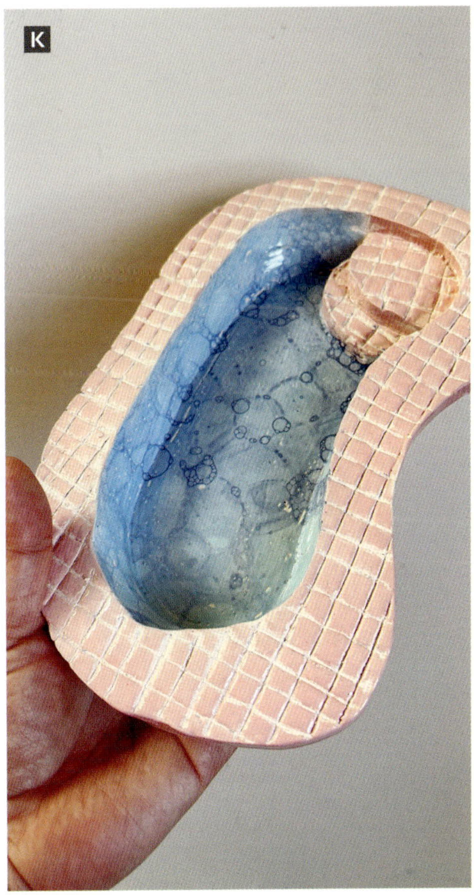
K

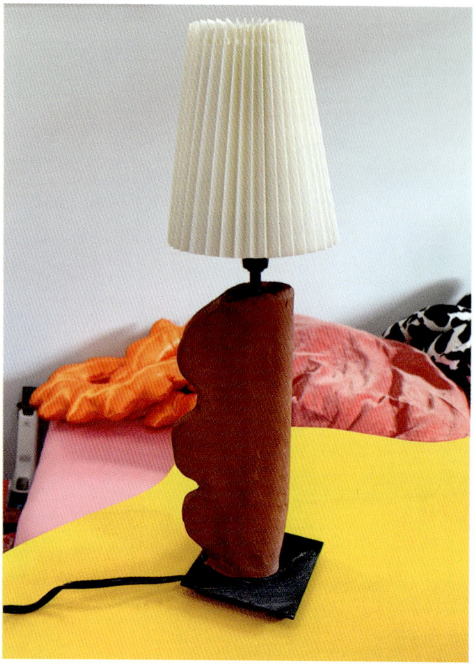

Upcycle Air-Dry Lamp

Use your slab skills to upcycle a lamp. You will need any working lamp base **A**. You can find them easily thrifting.

TOOLS

CLAY

ROLLING PIN

NEEDLE TOOL

LAMP BASE

WATER

SPONGE

1. Roll out a large slab of air-dried clay the height of the stem of the lamp **B**.
2. Create a cylinder around the lamp base with the clay without letting it touch the lamp's stem **C**. This clay will shrink so you won't want to put it directly around anything or it will crack.
3. Score and slip the slabs together **D**.
4. Trim the edges of the lamp to a fun shape.
5. Add whatever decorate bits you want to add. I've added texture to the surface of this piece **E**.

Note: Air-dry clay will stick to anything and everything once it's dry. Wipe down everything before its dries.

6. Air-dry clay doesn't need to be fired so let it dry and it will harden on its own.
7. Use acrylic paint to decorate as you wish.
8. Add a clear coat of acrylic or mod podge to seal in your piece and you're done!

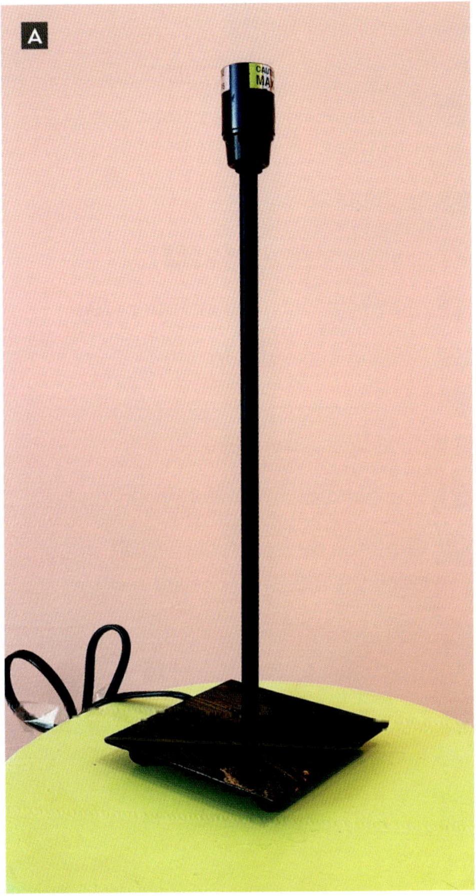
A

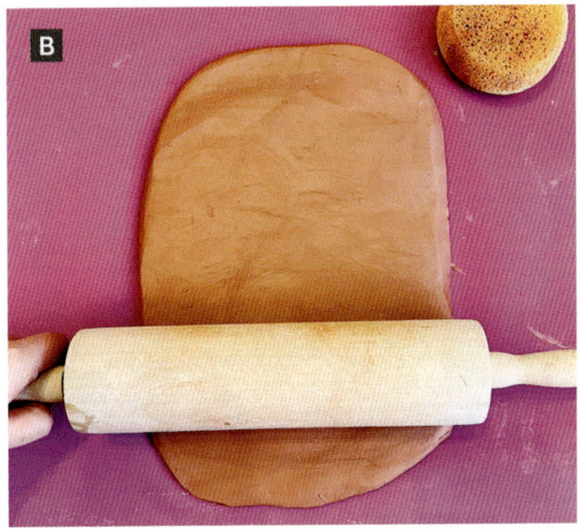
B

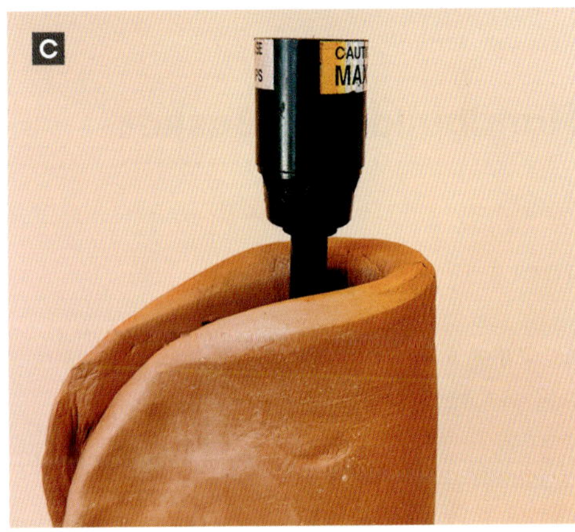
C

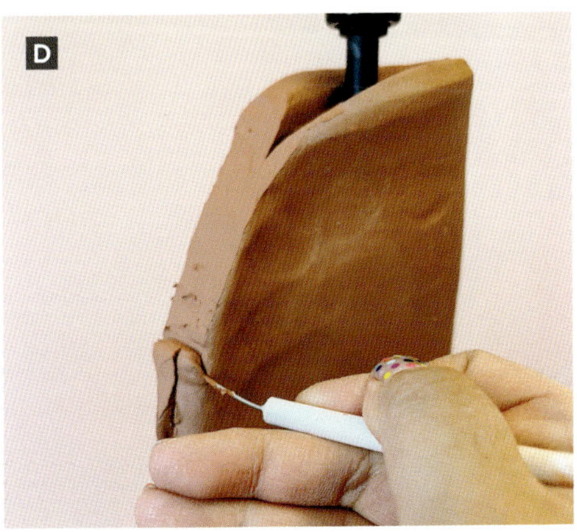
D

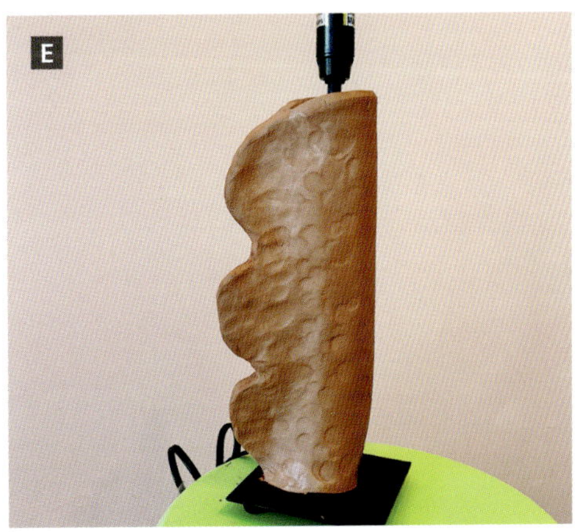
E

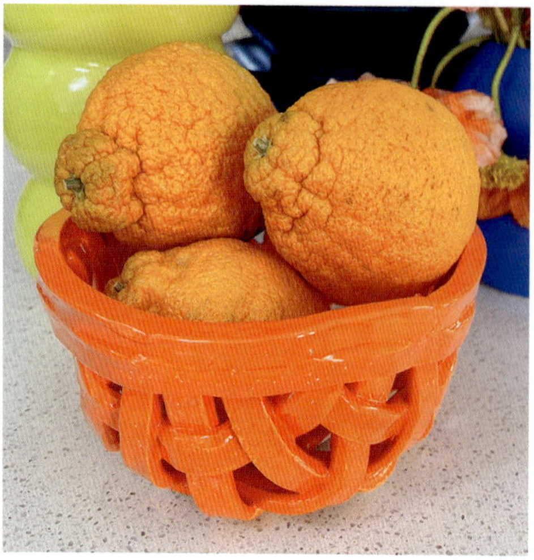

Handbuilding a Basket

Build a lovely fruit basket with your new skills!

TOOLS

CLAY
ROLLING PIN
NEEDLE TOOL
WATER
BOWL
TOWELS

1. Grab a bowl the size of the basket you want to make.
2. Line the inside of the bowl with wet paper towels.
3. Roll out two slabs.
4. Cut strips from the slab **A**.
5. Start with two horizontal strips **B**.
6. Add two vertical strips.
7. Lift the legs of the strips to create a simple basket pattern **C**.
8. Score and slip the meeting places.
9. Continue the basket pattern **D** and, once you reach the top, trim the excess clay.
10. Add one strip around the rim of the top edge to connect all the pieces **E**.
11. Let this basket slowly dry. Keep the piece wrapped with plastic overnight then loosely tent the piece with plastic for a week until the piece is fully dry. This piece will be very delicate.
12. Fire it and you're done!

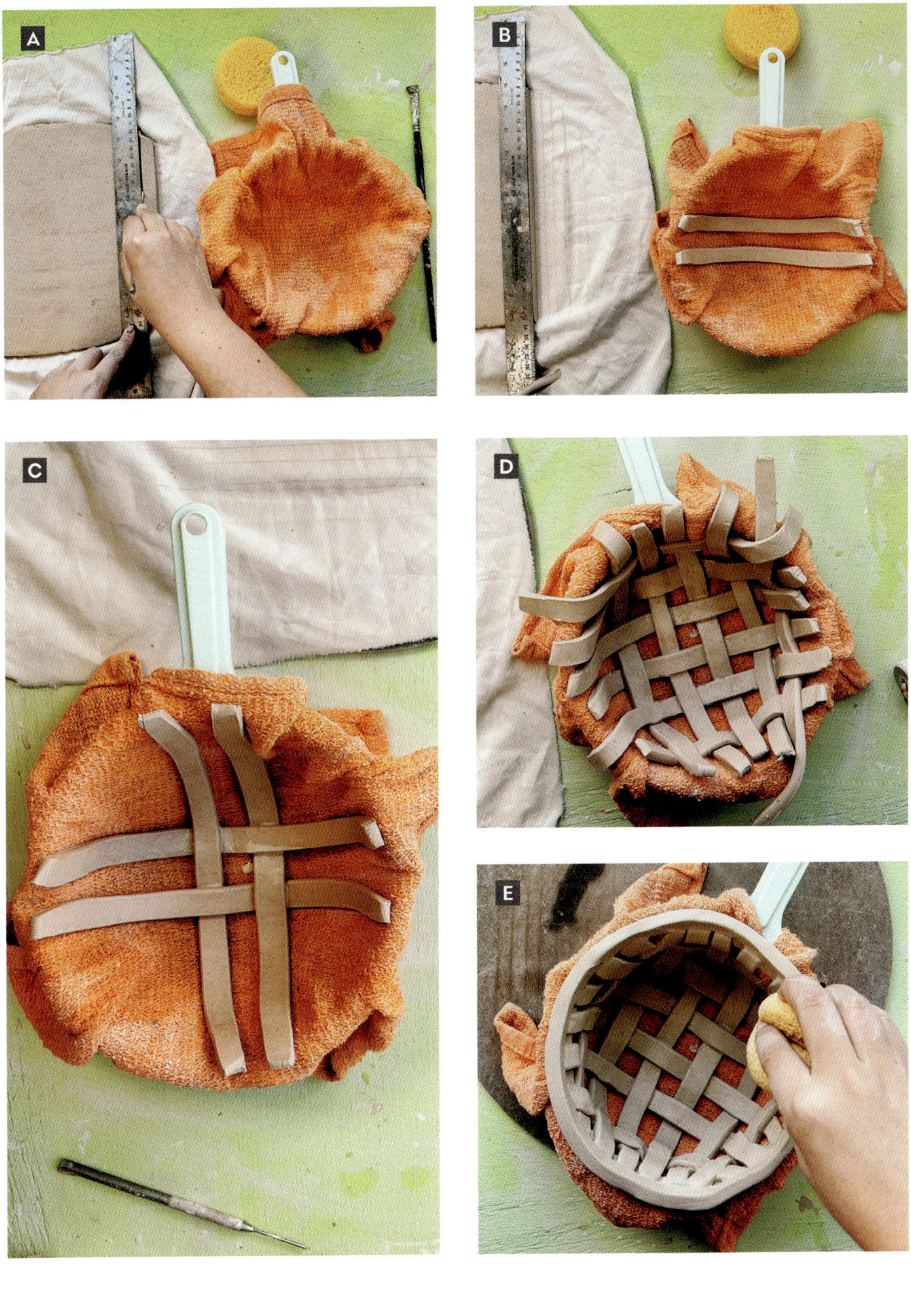
A
B
C
D
E

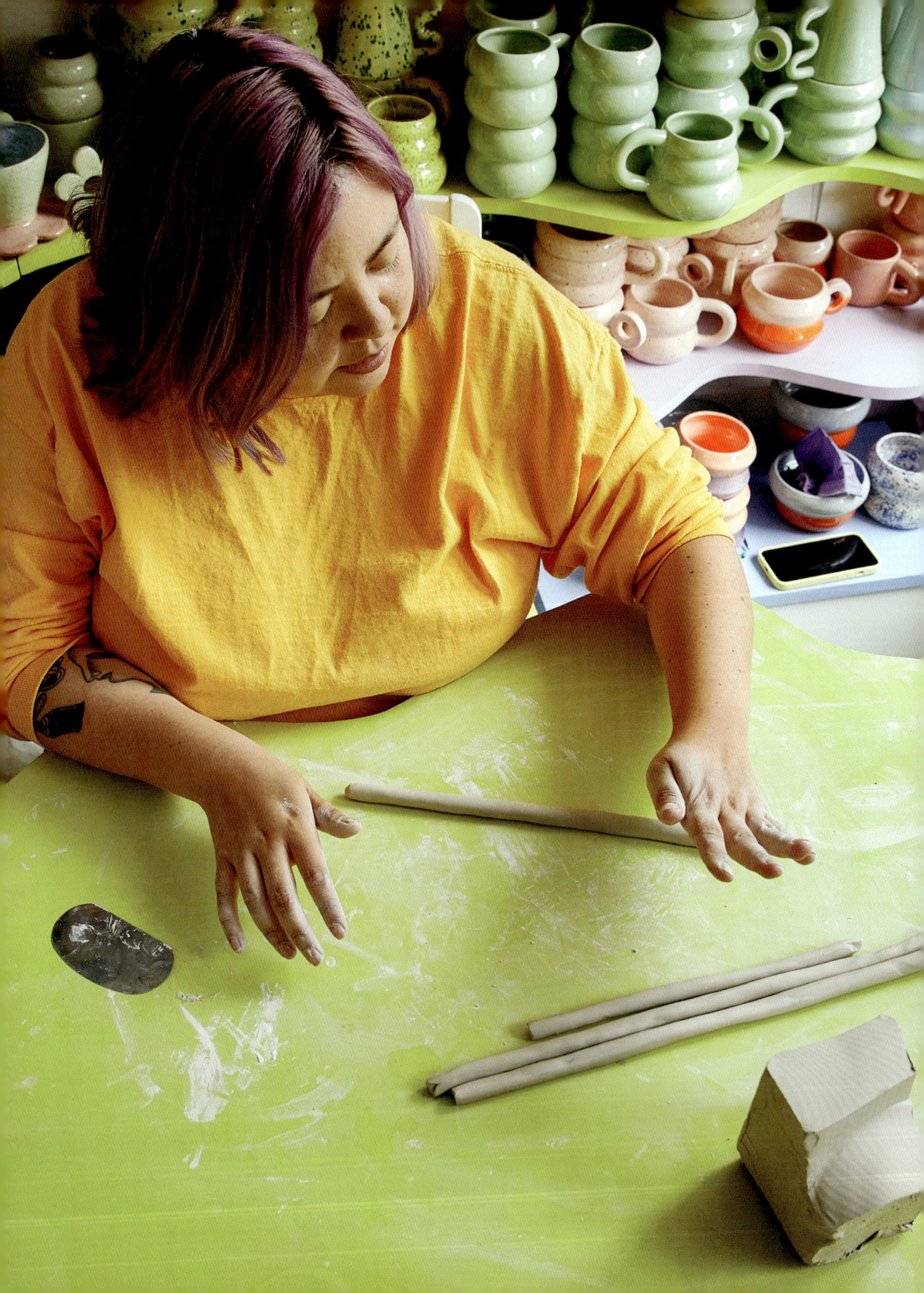

4

Coil Method

BASIC COIL METHOD
PAGE 60

HOW TO PULL A HANDLE
PAGE 62

HOW TO ATTACH A HANDLE
PAGE 62

CHAPTER 4

Coil Method

The coil method is used to create taller pieces that have challenging angles. It involves the rolling out of clay into long snake-like pieces and building height by adding to the circumference. This method has been used in many cultures. The coil method can be really fun. You can keep building and building your piece, and you can even invert your rim. This method is used in a lot of Native American, Mexican, and Greek pottery among many others. Making coils can be painstaking work and you need to keep them moist for them to be workable. Extruder to the rescue!

Key Terms

Dies: Metal or plastic plates, which the clay gets pressed through. Dies come in all shapes and sizes.

Extruders: These are like a big Play-Doh fun factory and literally extrudes clay through dies. Extruders come in gun form or wall extruders. The extruder guns are a lot like caulking guns and can make coils quickly. Wall extruders can pump out pounds of clay coils at a time.

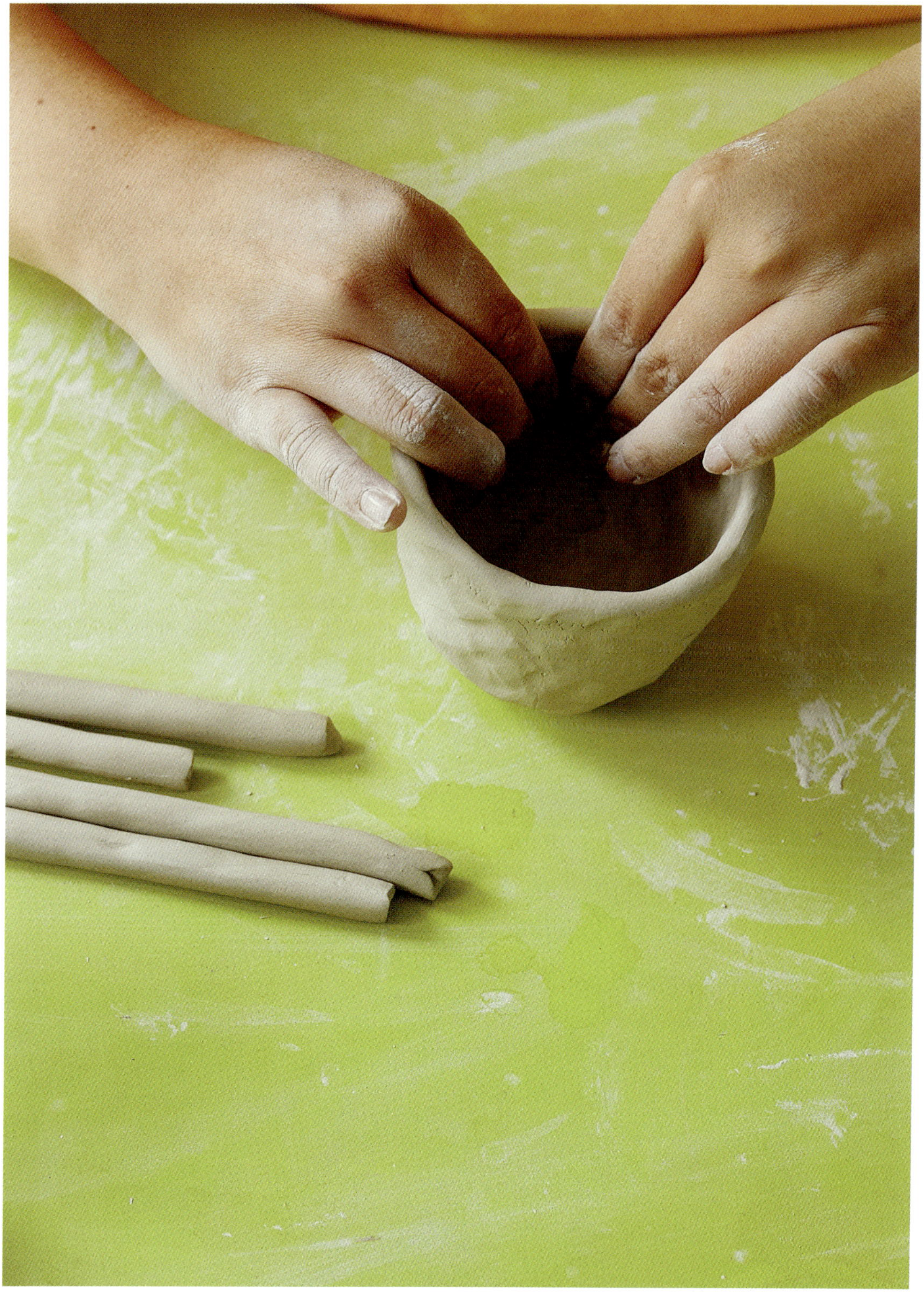

Basic Coil Method

Coil building is a fun way to gain height on a project without throwing on the wheel. Let's get started:

TOOLS

CLAY
CUTTING WIRE
POROUS SURFACE
WOOD SMOOTHING TOOL
PLASTIC BAGS

1. Prepare a small ball of clay. Using your palms, roll out the clay against the table until it becomes a long snake-like shape. These will be the coils **A**. It's tempting to roll the clay out with your fingers, but don't, you will end up with a bumpy witch's wand shape. The clay needs to stay compressed to prevent cracking and to hold its structure and working on a table will help with this.

2. Make about five coils at about 12 inches each and keep them covered in plastic to keep them moist.

3. Start by making a pinch pot base. The rim on this pinch pot should be about as thick as your coil. Start lining the rim of the pinch pot with coils **B**. No need to score and slip! With every coil placed, apply pressure and smooth out the seams on both inner and outer surfaces **C** **D** **E**.

4. Keep adding coils until your piece is as tall as you want **F**. You might need to periodically spray the piece with water to keep it moist.

5. Once the piece is fully dry, send it to be fired!

Coil building can be a great way to gain height if you are not yet proficient with wheel throwing. Some potters use coil building in addition to throwing by adding coils to a thrown base and building height that way. This is a great technique to use if you don't have the arm strength to throw big.

Note: Coil-built pieces need to be dried slowly to prevent cracking by loosely covering the piece with plastic.

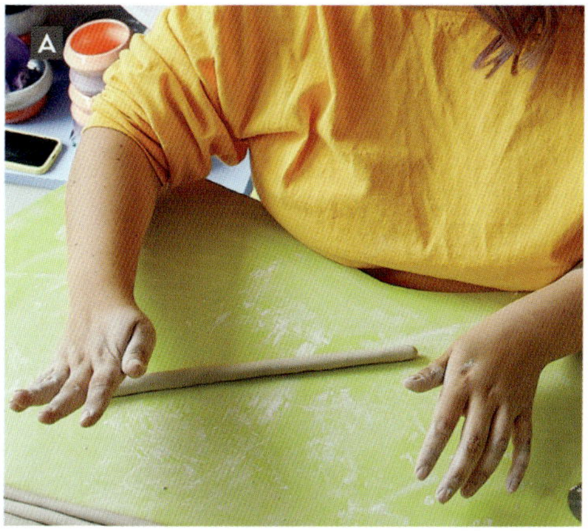
A

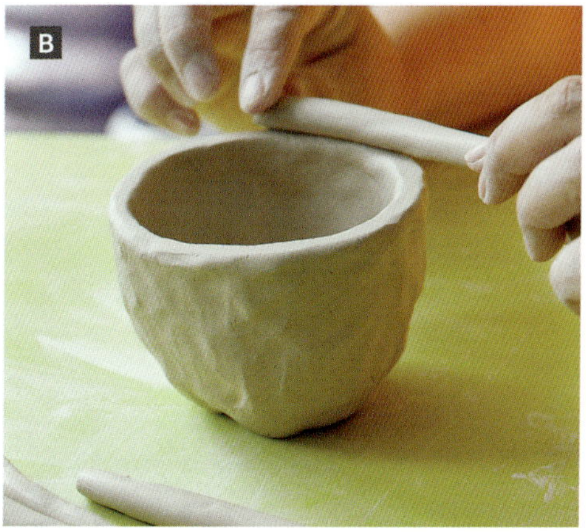
B

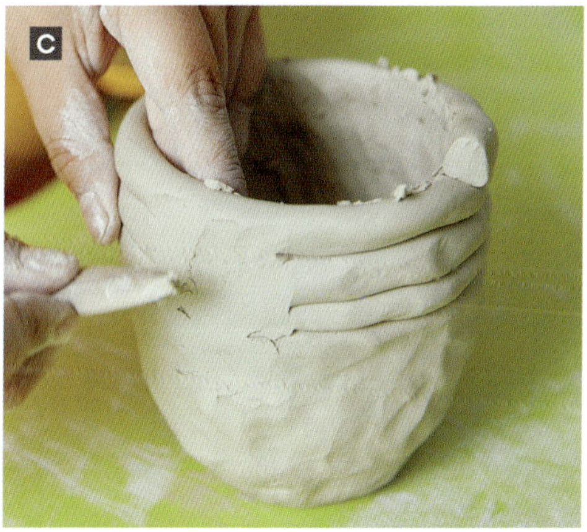
C

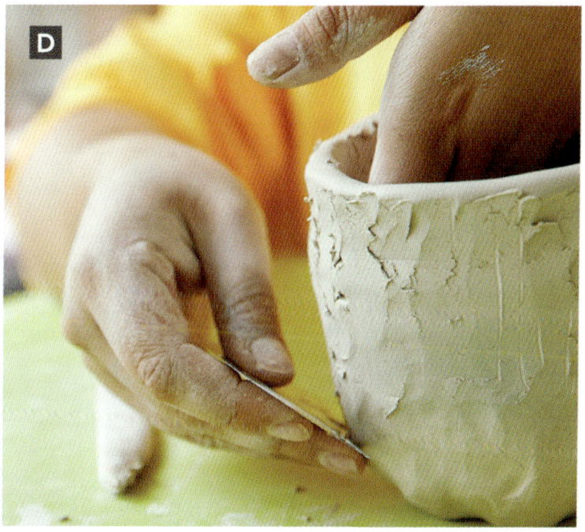
D

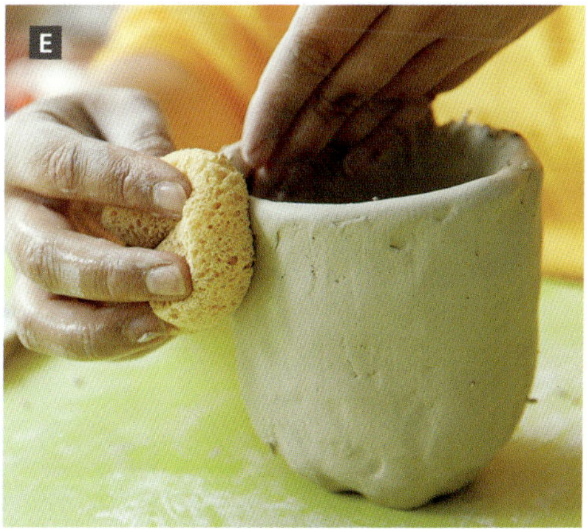
E

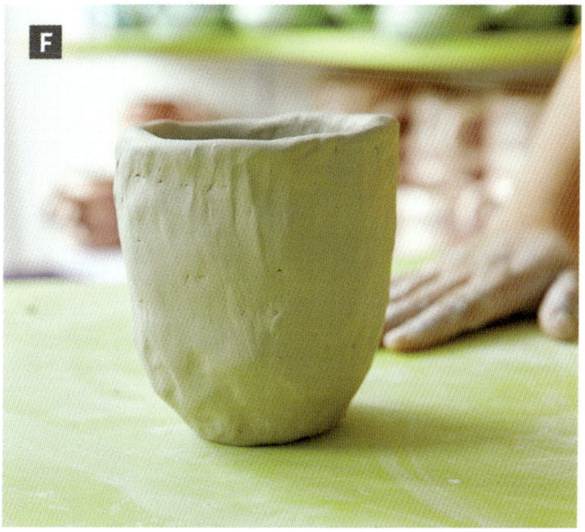
F

How to Pull a Handle

Handles come in all shapes and sizes. Pulling handles is common with production potters because it's easy to make many at once.

1 Take a ball of clay and roll it into a cucumber shaped form **A**.

2 Grab a bowl of water.

3 Hold the clay with your non-dominant hand and use your dominant hand to wet the end of the clay.

4 Start pulling by putting your hand at the bottom third of the clay and pull down gently.

5 Keep pulling while keeping your hands and clay very wet. The motion should be like milking a cow.

6 Once you have a desired length, pinch it off **B**, shape it into an arch for your handle, and then let it sit until it is almost leather hard **C**.

How to Attach a Handle

1 Mark where you want the handle to be attached and score both the vessel and the handle at attachment points **D**.

2 Apply slip to both surfaces at the meeting points.

3 Attach the handle and apply pressure to the meeting points by pressing from the inside of the vessel toward the handle outside **E**.

4 Smooth out the meeting points of the attachments.

5 You can now set up the piece to dry **F**. When you have attachments, the handle and vessel might be at different levels of dryness. To make your piece dry evenly, drape the piece with a sheet of plastic and leave it for a day then open it up a bit to dry out. The pieces have to be at a similar level of dryness because as the clay shrinks, if they are at different levels of dryness, the attachments will crack or break off.

We will explore how to fire your piece in a kiln in the next chapter!

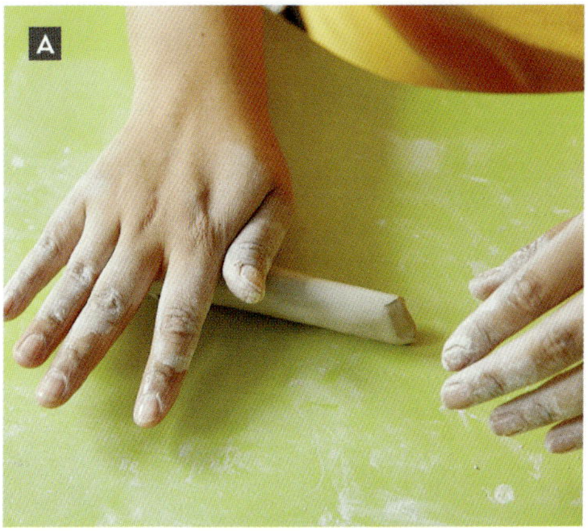
A

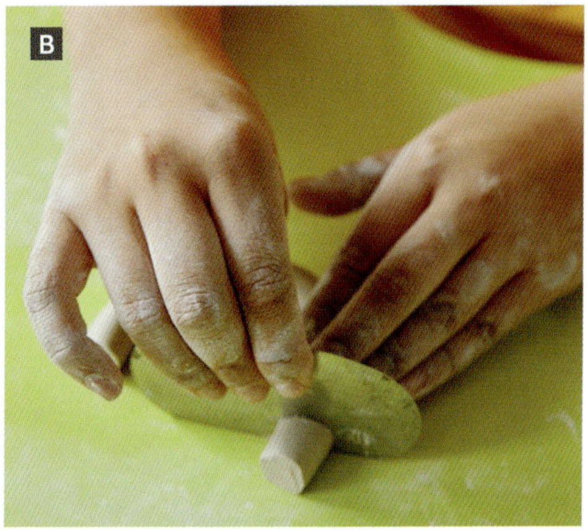
B

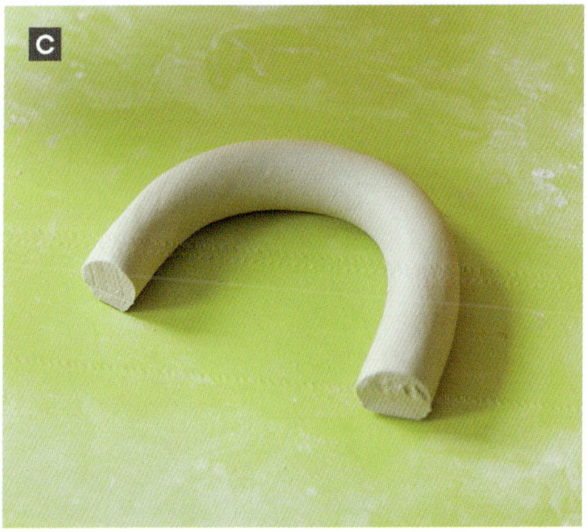
C

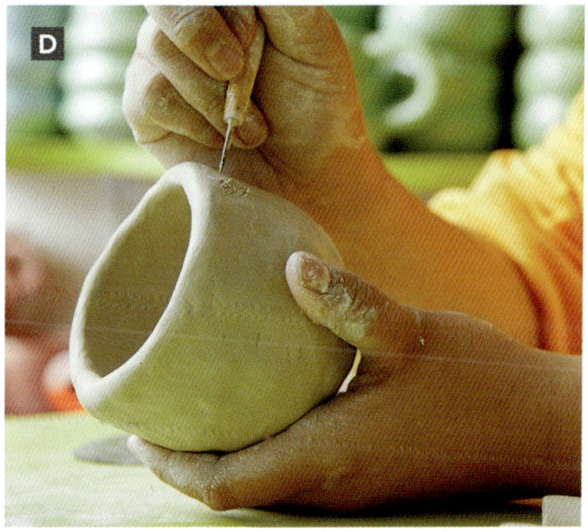
D

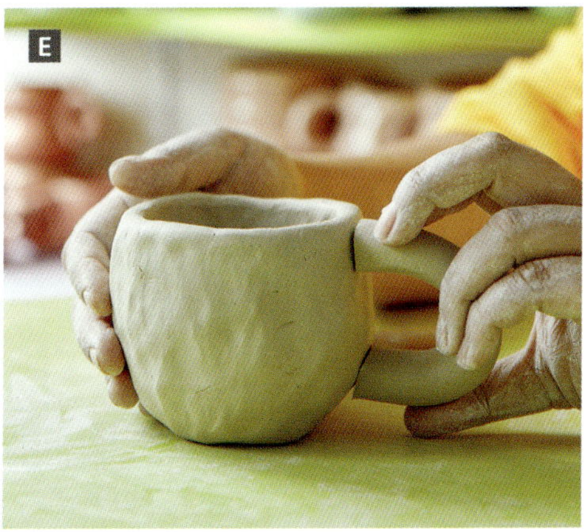
E

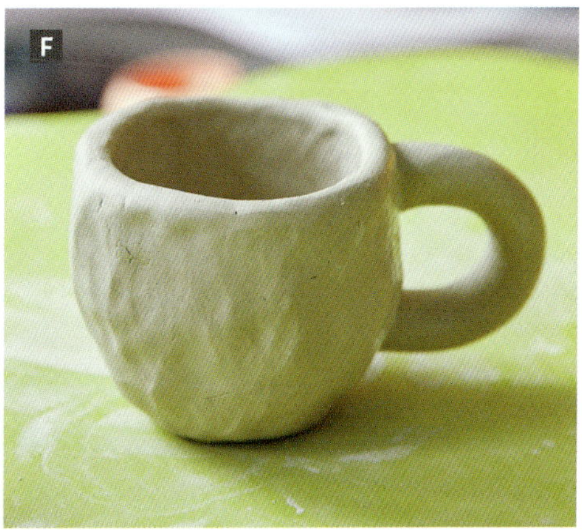
F

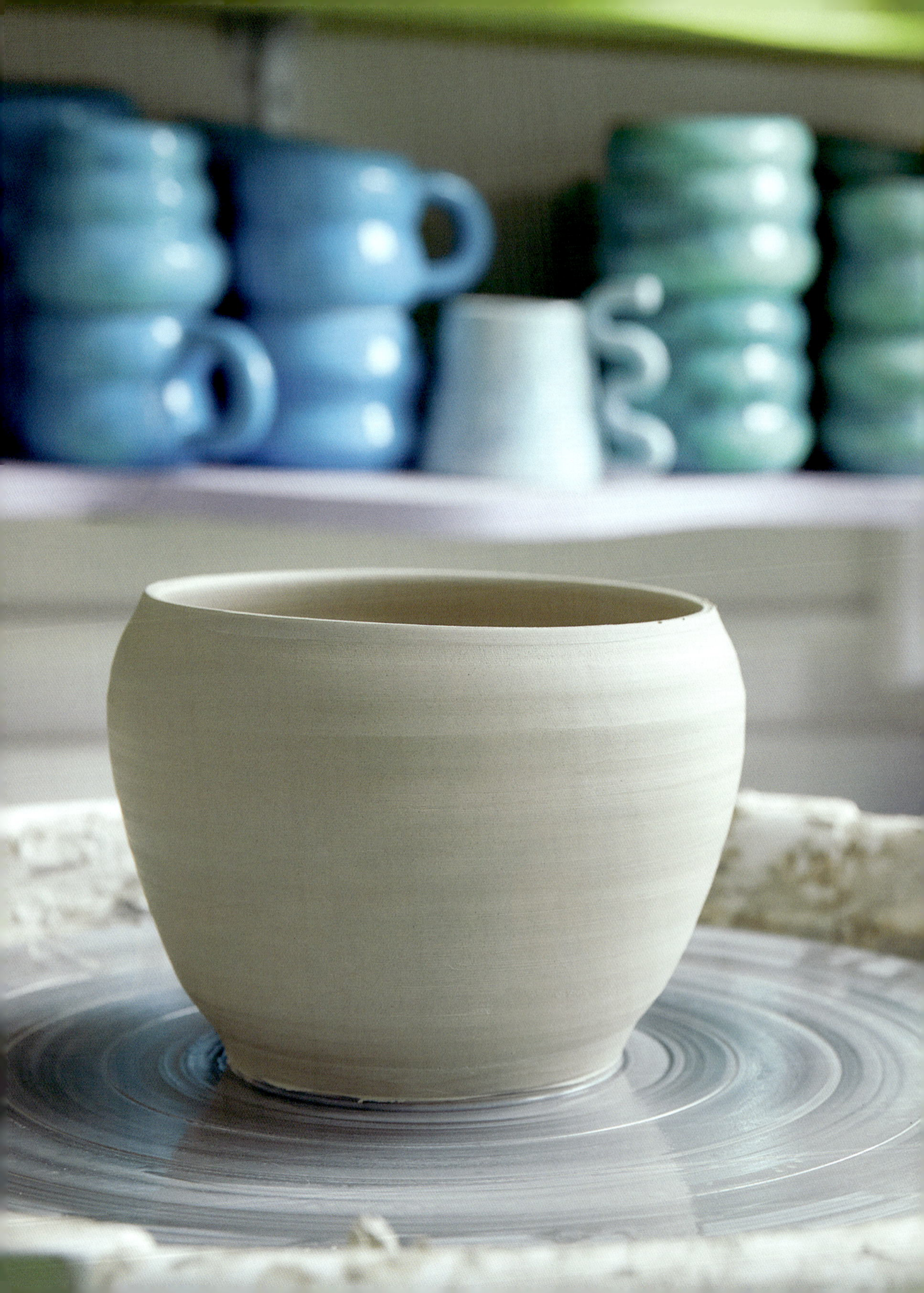

Wheel Throwing

GETTING STARTED
PAGE 68

WIRING OFF
PAGE 72

TRIMMING THE FOOT
PAGE 72

CHAPTER 5

Wheel Throwing

This is a biggie. Wheel throwing isn't easy, and some people struggle with it for years. But there's no need to become discouraged! There are tips you can pick up to make your journey on the wheel easier.

Key Terms

Bat: Portable work surface for clay pieces. Bats can be attached to a wheel to help lift delicate or heavy pieces off the wheel without warping the piece. A bat looks like a presswood piece that fits on top of the wheel and fits into the pins that protrude from the wheelhead.

Compressing: When you apply firm pressure to the clay, either with a tool or with your finger. This tightens up the clay by compressing the particles of clay together.

Throwing: The process of creating pottery pieces on a wheel.

Wheel: A pottery wheel is a machine used to center and shape clay. It has a circular wheel head that spins while the potter can use both hands to shape the clay.

Wheelhead: The flat disc on a potter's wheel that you throw on.

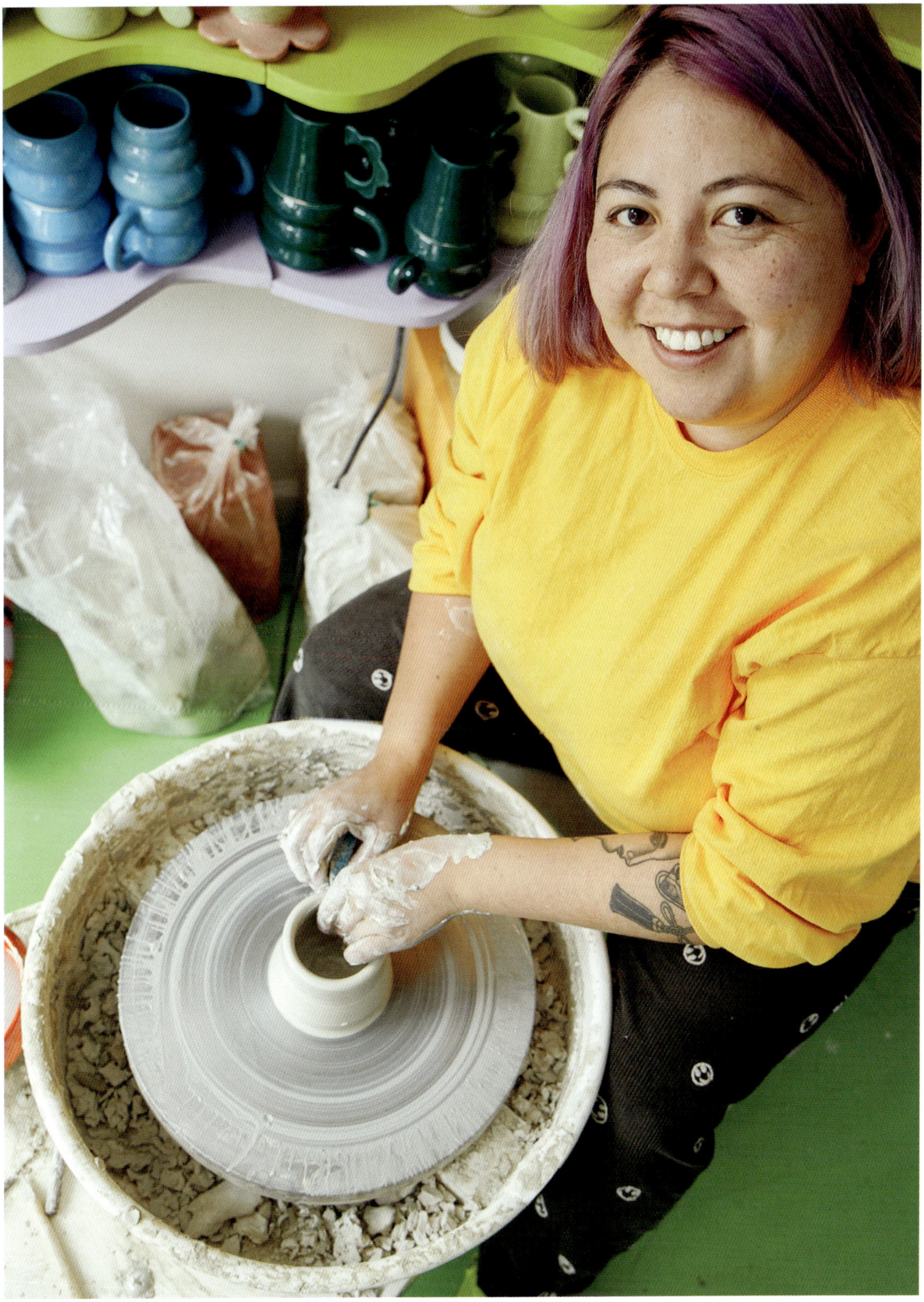

Getting Started

Throwing can be frustrating because it involves a lot of coordination. Let's start with an easy mug project to get used to the process.

The first step in the process of throwing is to get your clay properly positioned on the wheel and getting it to stick on the surface. Sealing clay to the wheelhead is important because, if you don't, the clay will fall off the wheel head while throwing.

TOOLS

CLAY
CUTTING WIRE
WOOD RIB
NEEDLE TOOL
SPONGE
RUBBER RIB

Following are the first steps in the process:

1 Start by making a manageable ball of clay about the size of a peach **A**.

2 Find the center of your wheel. Aim and throw the clay in the center. This might take a few tries, but you do need to throw it with some force for it to stick to the wheel or bat. For added adhesion I smooth out the edges of the clay to the wheelhead **B**.

3 Add a bit of water **C** and start rotating the wheel slowly and then begin to seal the clay on the wheelhead dragging your finger along the edge at the base of the clay **D**.

4 Cup the clay on the wheel like the motion of holding a ladybug in your hand, making sure your fingers cross each other and aren't in a praying position **E**. You are throwing with your palms not your fingers.

CENTERING

Centering your clay on the wheel is probably the most difficult thing about throwing for a beginner. You are basically working with the centrifugal force of the wheel to make the clay even all around as well as wedging the clay on the wheel, centering it inside and out.

Here are the next steps in the process:

1 After the clay has been secured and sealed on the wheelhead, increase the speed of the wheel a bit. The pace should be similar to a bike cruising on the beach—not speeding—just cruising.

2 Keep your non-dominant hand cupped around the side of the clay and use your dominant hand to make a slow chopping motion to flatten the top of the clay **F**. Press down firmly and be mindful that you are throwing with your entire body, not your wrists.

3 Squeeze the clay upward with even pressure to create a pillar and then chop down to create a plateau on top. Repeat this process as many times as it takes until you notice the clay is even all around.

Note: It's less about seeing that it's even all around and more about feeling that the clay is even. Look away from the clay and feel if the clay is off. I usually don't look at the clay at all when I'm centering because it throws me off. It's like learning to ride a bike and looking down versus looking forward.

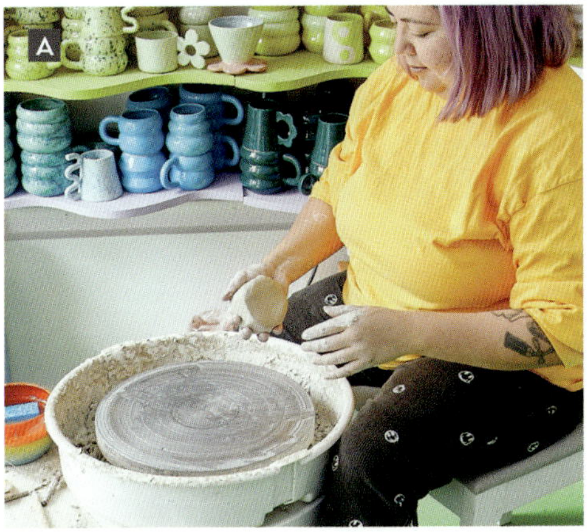
A

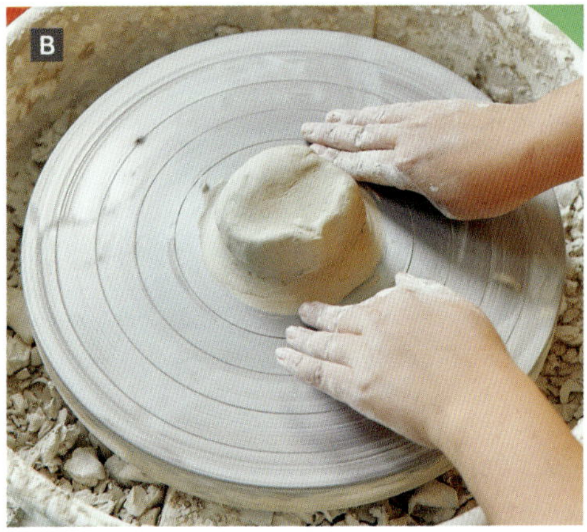
B

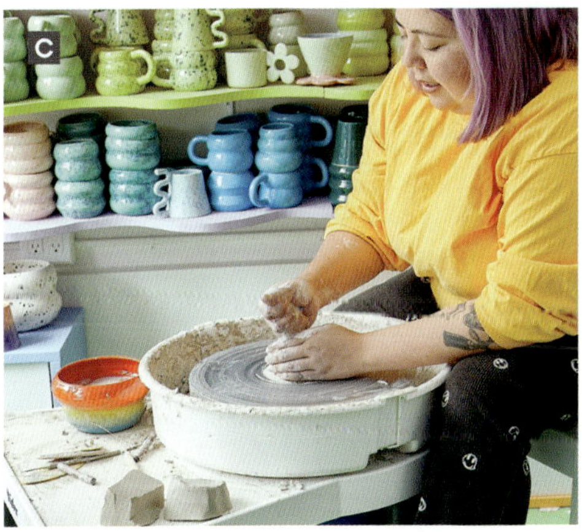
C

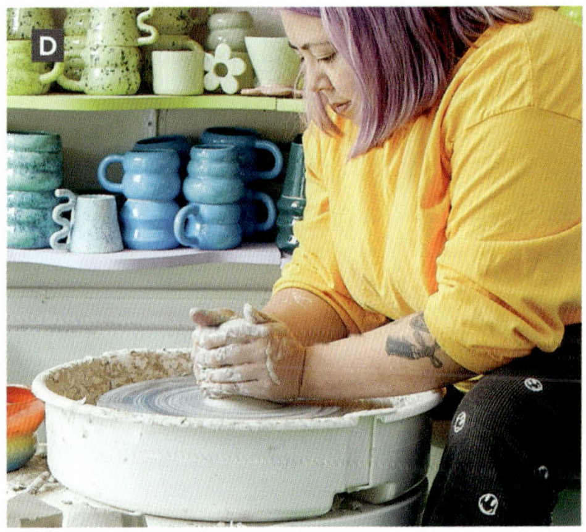
D

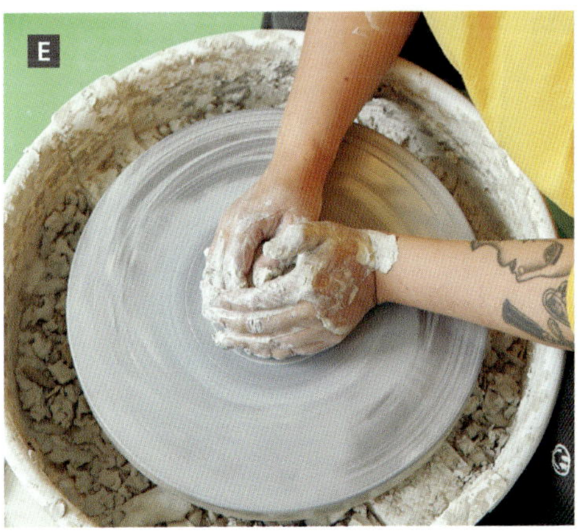
E

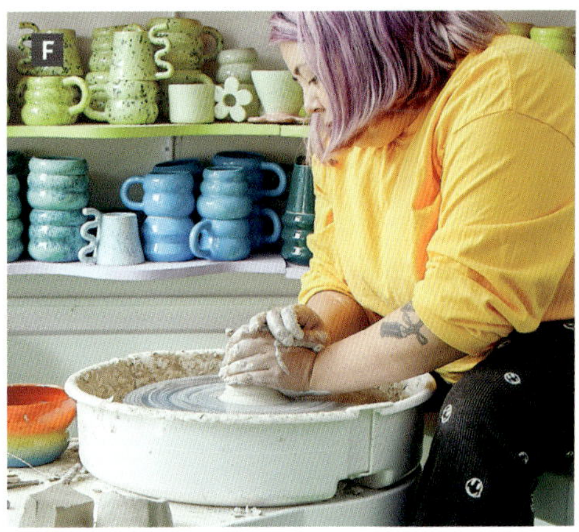
F

Don't skip truly centering the clay. It's not possible to create a symmetrical pot without first centering. If you don't, you'll struggle throughout the whole process.

OPENING UP

After your clay has been sealed and properly centered, the next steps will take you through the process of opening it up:

1 While the wheel is still spinning at "cruising" speed, make a divot in the center top (the plateau) of your clay lump **G**. The spinning of the clay will guide your finger to the center to make the divot. Again, this step is more about feeling than looking for the center.

2 Dip your finger down slowly until you can estimate the thickness of the bottom of your vessel. This will take some practice **H**.

3 If you are nearing what you think should be the thickness of the base, you can test the thickness! Bring the wheel to a complete stop. Take your needle tool and put your finger toward the end of it leaving the tip exposed about an inch. Poke the needle tool straight down to the center of the piece until you hit the wheelhead, then slide your finger down to where the clay is. When you pull out the needle you will now have the measurement of the thickness of the base from your fingertip to the end of the needle tool.

4 If you're satisfied with the thickness, which should be about half an inch, make sure you compress and close up the hole.

PULLING UP THE WALLS

Once you've opened up the clay you can start to pull the walls up to get some height and get rid of bulk. Slow the wheel down to two-thirds the pace and follow these steps:

1 Place your finger from your non-dominant hand in the inside of the piece at the very bottom. Place a finger from your dominant hand on the outside above where the other finger is **I**. Picture that the clay will be shaped into a letter "S" and your fingers are in the divots of the letter.

2 Now slowly pull both hands up in a pace of one second—or "one Mississippi"—per inch. I know that's a weird metric, but the pace is important for keeping the walls even. The amount of pressure is about the pressure you would use when testing the ripeness of an avocado. As you throw more, you can figure out what pressure is good for you but for now start with light pressure.

3 Keep pulling walls until they are ⅓-inch thick **J**.

4 Compress the rim every time you pull the wall up **K** **L**.

5 Also compress the inside with a dry sponge and make sure there is no water at the bottom of the vessel, or you will get an "S" crack, which is exactly what it sounds like; a crack shaped like an "S" that happens due to excess moisture. By now you should start seeing a mug begin to form.

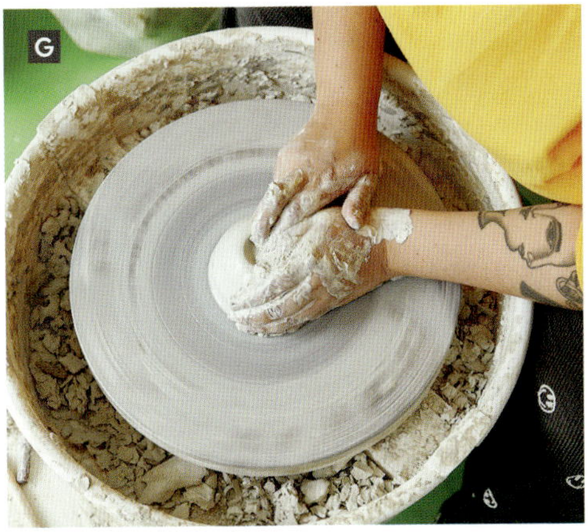
G

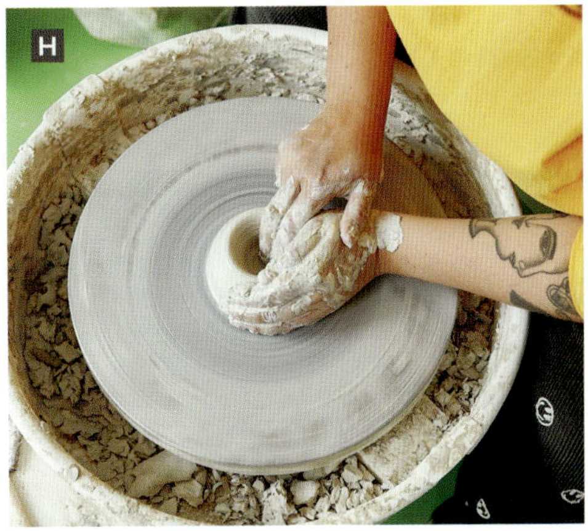
H

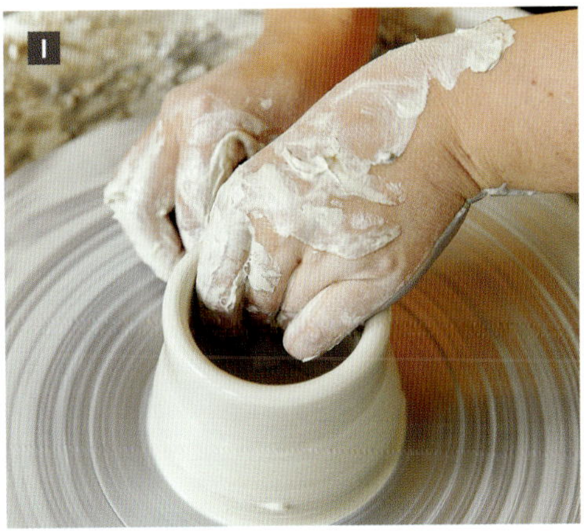
I

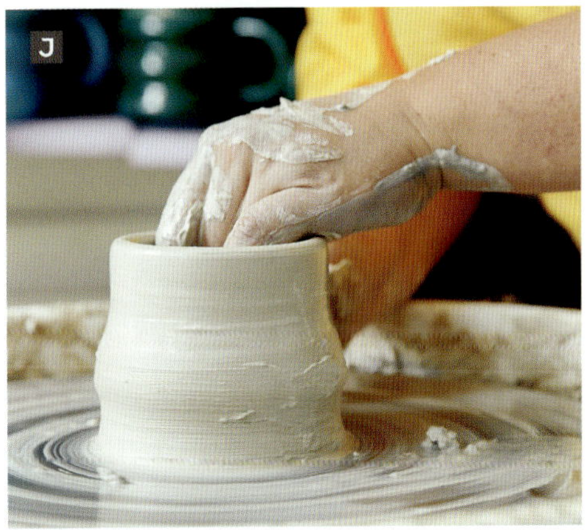
J

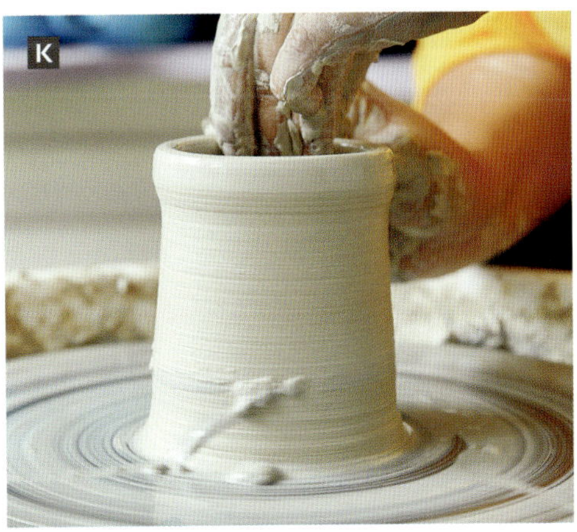
K

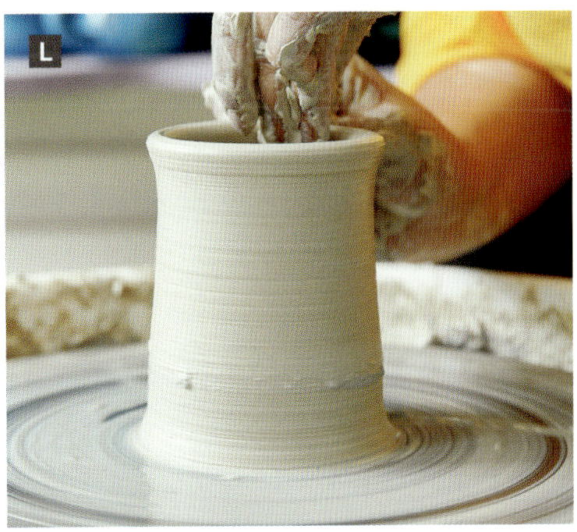
L

Wiring Off

Next you will need to cut the vessel off the wheel, which can take some practice. Follow the steps below:

1. Take your cutting wire and pull it taught, then graze it against the surface of the wheel under the piece to slice off your creation **A**.

2. With open hands so you don't dent the bottom, slightly twist the piece, lift, and place it on a wooden board where it will stay until it is dried to a leather-hard state.

Trimming the Foot

The foot is the bottom of your piece. Some are flat or have a trimmed lip at the bottom.

Once your piece has dried to the leather-hard stage, you can trim the foot. Follow these steps:

1. Flip your piece over and place it in the center of the wheelhead.

2. Gently attach the rim of the piece with three pieces of fresh clay pressed to the sides securing it to the wheelhead **B**.

3. Use your needle tool to mark where you want to trim off material to make the foot. Turn the wheel as slow as possible.

4. Use your finger from your non-dominant hand to find the center of your piece, hold down the piece at this spot.

5. Use your larger trim tools to cut the bulk and the smaller trim tools to refine the foot **C**.

Note: If your piece has a narrow neck that won't stand on the wheel, you can use a chuck. A chuck is a tool that will elevate your piece so you can trim the foot without distorting the top of your pot. You can throw a chuck on the wheel and bisque it or you can use a found object like a coffee can.

The leather-hard stage is a great time to add attachments and decorative elements. If you're making a mug, this would be the time to attach a handle. You can cut a slab to make a handle, roll out a coil handle, or pull handles.

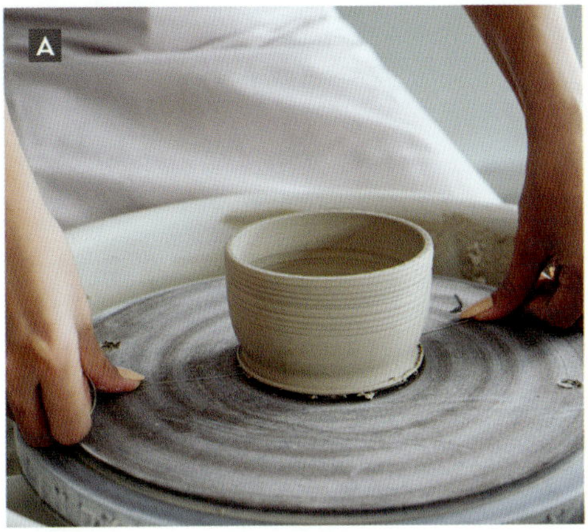
A

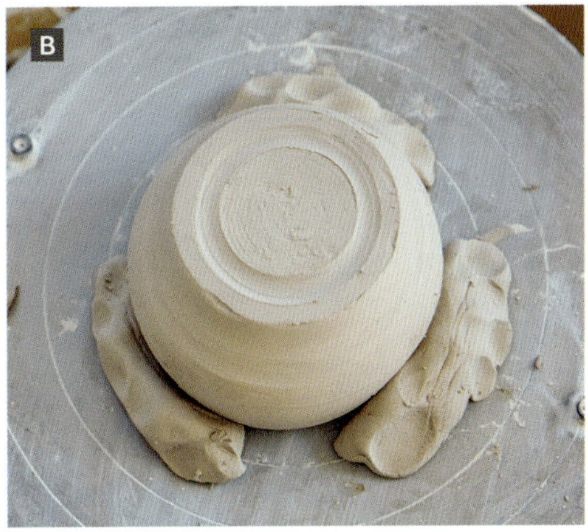
B

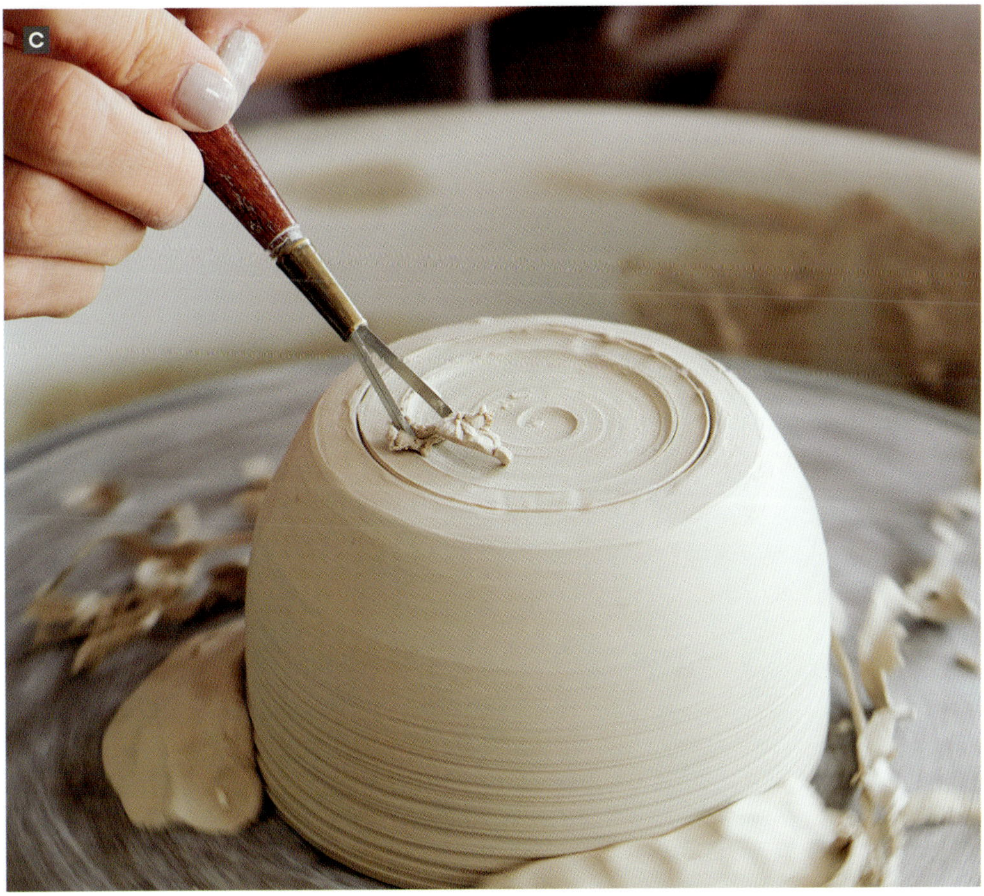
C

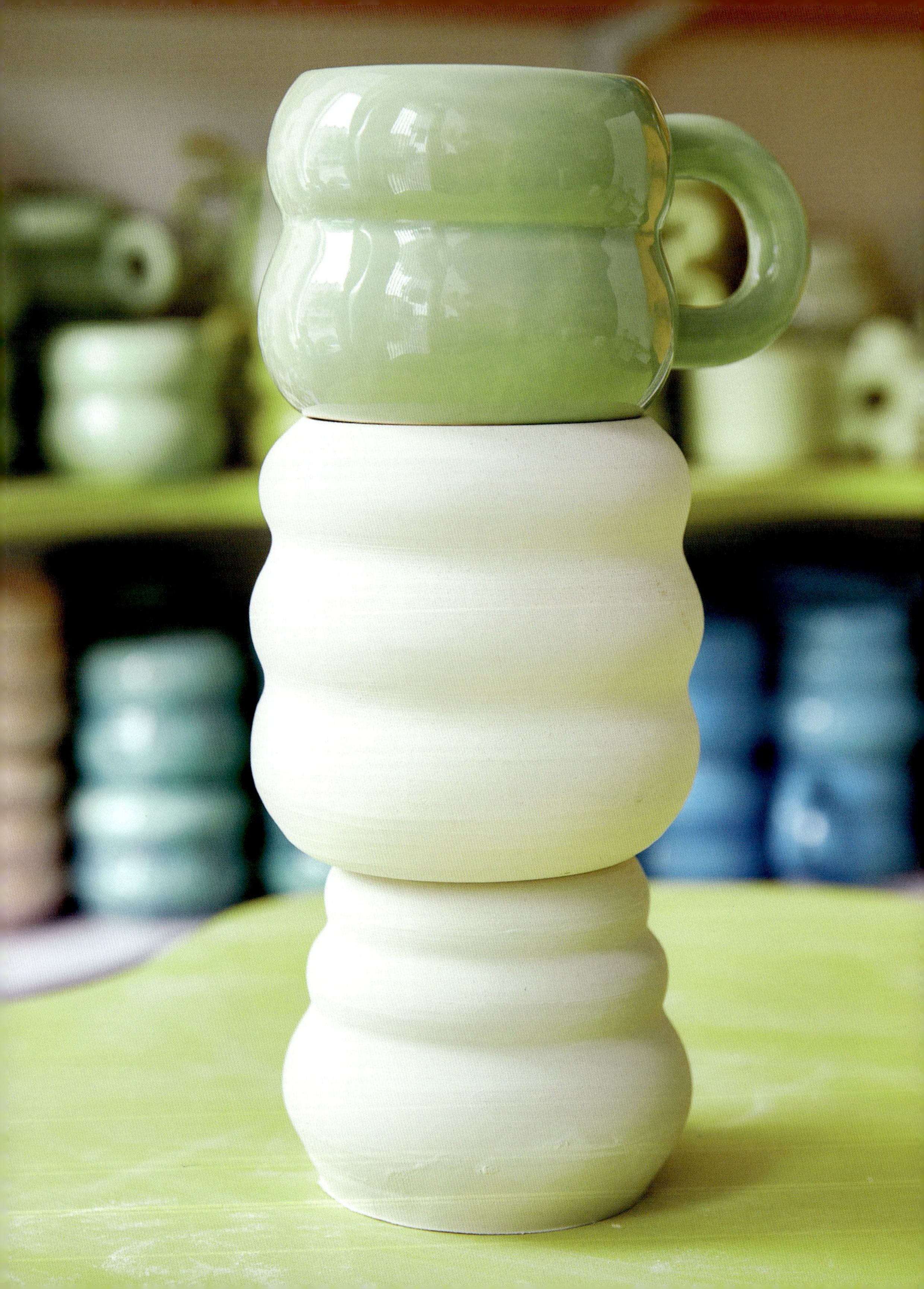

Finishing and Firing

CHAPTER 6

Finishing and Firing

Whether pinch pot or wheel thrown, slab built, or coil constructed, you have many options for decorative finishing and firings. The options depend on the stage of clay, the type of clay, and the type of firing. You can decorate during the leather-hard stage, on bisqueware, or during a special firing. Standard finishing for pottery is a bisque firing followed by a glaze firing but that's not a hard-and-fast rule. As you progress in your pottery education you will learn more and more about the possibilities.

Key Terms

Colored slip: Colored slip is made from slip and a mason stain, which is a colorant for ceramics, and can be applied to your piece at the leather-hard stage.

Decorative sgraffito: A technique for decorating leather-hard clay.

Glaze: A layer painted onto your piece that fuses in the firing process.

Underglaze: A type of decorative paint you can apply under the glaze of your piece.

Wax resist: Material used to prevent liquids, such as raw liquid glazes, from adhering to the clay.

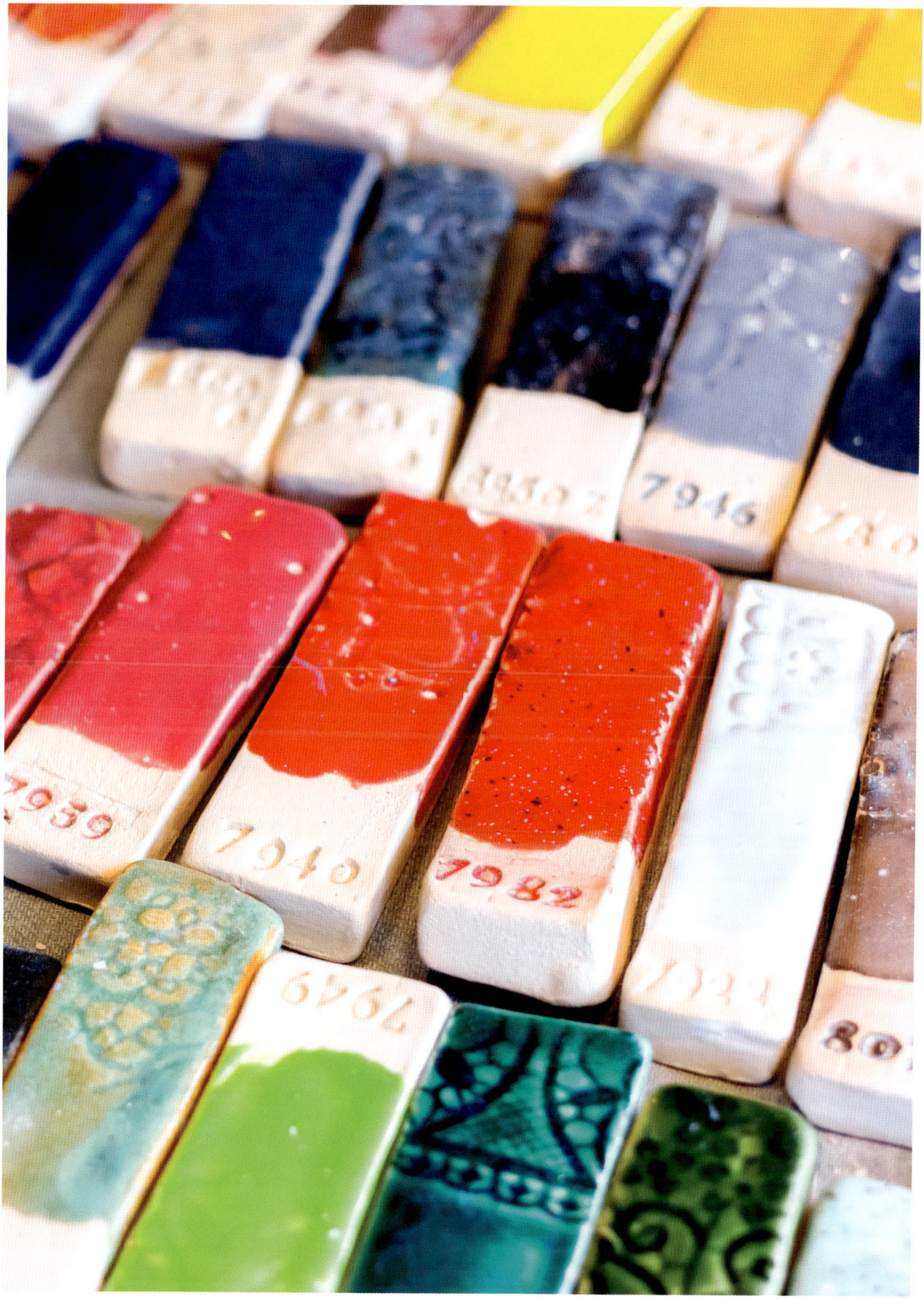
7946
7959
7940
7982
7949

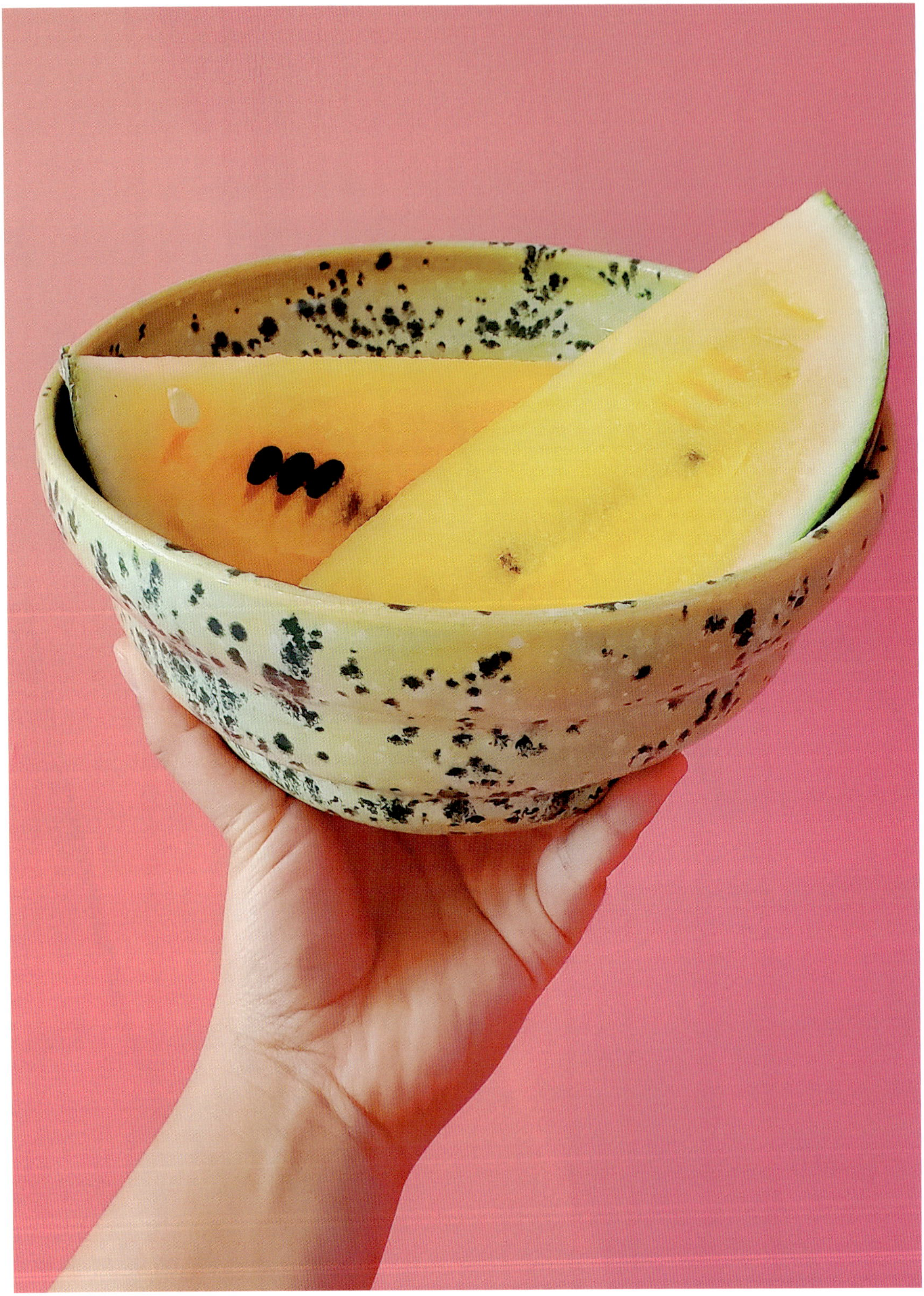

Decorating Before Firing

These are ways to decorate your piece when it's at the leather-hard stage so we will discuss several options.

COLORED SLIP

You can use colored slip as you would paint. You might need multiple layers to make the artwork opaque. Also, since you're using slip, whatever 3D elements you add (such as chunky brush strokes) will show up in the firing. Do not apply slip to greenware or bisque or it will flake off. Paint a coat of clear glaze after bisque over your decoration to become food safe.

DECORATIVE SGRAFFITO

Leather-hard clay can be decorated using the sgraffito technique. See page 88 for an example of how to do this process.

UNDERGLAZE

Underglaze is the easiest decorative element to work with. Underglazes are often used in children's art classes. Underglazes are not quite slip nor do they have the rigid rules of glaze. If you accidentally leave underglaze at the bottom of your piece, it's alright! Underglaze, like slip, will need a coat of clear glaze over it to be food safe.

BISQUE FIRE

When your pieces are finally at the bone-dry phase you can send them into the first firing. During the firing, the pieces go through stress because of the extreme heat. Sometimes you'll notice torquing, which is when the clay's memory is having its moment and can result in a plate that looks like a wave. Sometimes cracks that didn't show up on greenware will show up on bisque. The thing about cracks in pottery is that they get worse the higher the temperature in firings, so if the crack is noticeable at bisque, it will become worse after the final firing. If you have a small crack and you're determined to fix it, you can buy a mender that mixes with the slip of the clay you're using. Apply this mix heavily over the crack. If there's extra mender after it has been fired, you can sand it off.

GLAZE

Glazing can add color and texture to your piece. There is a huge range of commercial glazes out there. Some are matte, some are glossy, some are metallic or opalescent, and some are textured. There are crawling glazes that give your piece a cobblestone texture. There are glazes that crackle intentionally, giving a beautiful rustic look to a piece. When choosing a glaze keep in mind the purpose of the piece. If you're making a mug or something that will be used for food, the glaze must be food-safe certified, not just non-toxic. Every glaze you pick will come with directions for how to apply it and its assigned cone temperature.

WAX IT

There needs to be no glaze at the bottom or ¼ inch from the bottom. If you leave glaze at the bottom of the piece, it will stick to the kiln shelf. Glaze can be difficult to remove so here comes wax resist to make your life a little easier. Wax resist is an interesting substance. You can add water to thin it out when it's in liquid form; if you let it dry it becomes a solid.

Follow these simple steps:

1. Apply just one coat of wax resist to the bottom of your piece with your wax-dedicated brush.
2. Glaze it! Then wipe off the glaze that is sitting on the wax. The wax makes it easier to remove the glaze from the surface. After you remove the glaze from the bottom, you're ready to fire it.
3. Be careful with the wax, if you make a mistake and splash it on your pot you will be unable to take it off without another firing.

Note: You can brush on shapes to your piece with wax resist, glaze it, and then remove the excess to reveal a fun decoration.

BRUSH GLAZE

Brushing on glaze can be very meditative and it is a slow process. Usually, it's recommended to brush on two-to-three layers of glaze if you want the glaze to be opaque. Make your brush strokes as even as possible to avoid visible streaks and wait for the layers to dry between applications.

DIP GLAZE

Dip glazes are usually found at shared studios. The length of time you dip a piece will determine the thickness of the glaze, so don't dip them too long or the glaze will run onto the kiln shelves during firing.

SPRAY GLAZE

You can spray glaze onto a piece in a spray booth. The spray booth has a glaze spray gun that you can put thinned-out glaze in and the booth itself has a vented hood and fan to remove the excess glaze in the air. Sprayed-on glaze will add a beautiful blush to your piece. The downside is that spraying requires a lot of equipment. Glaze booths, spray guns, and air compressors can get pricey.

LAYERING

You can layer glazes to achieve some really cool effects. For example, you can dip half of a plate in red glaze, the other half in blue, and where the two colors meet there will be a mix of both creating a beautiful purple.

GLAZE FIRING

There are many different ways of firing pottery. The most popular is cone 5 electric firing because it's very consistent and it's simple to set the kiln. Read the labels on your glaze before firing. Generally, when you're starting out you have little to no control over the actual firing process: you are usually working in a group studio where it isn't appropriate to ask for a different firing that might affect other people's work in the kiln.

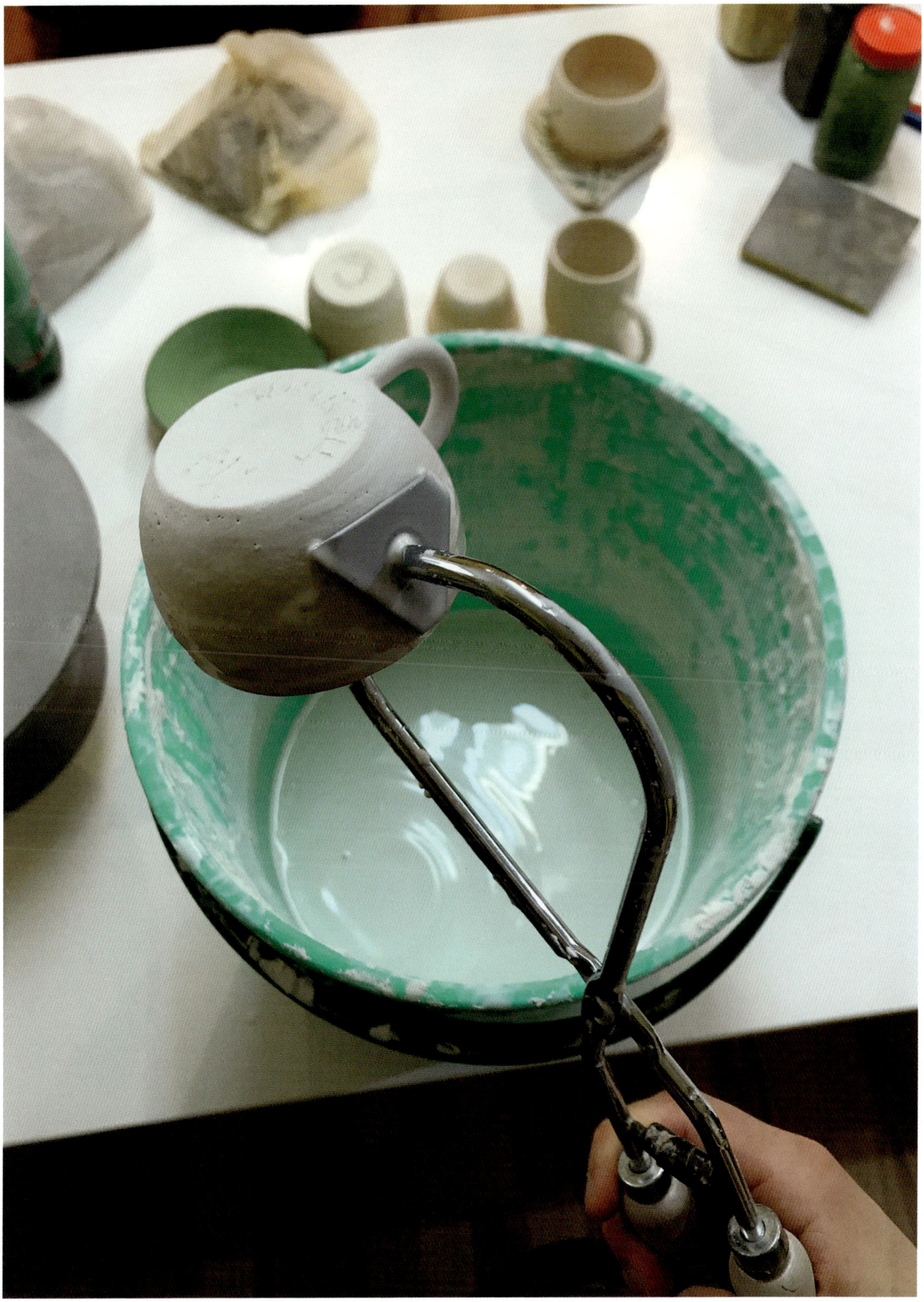

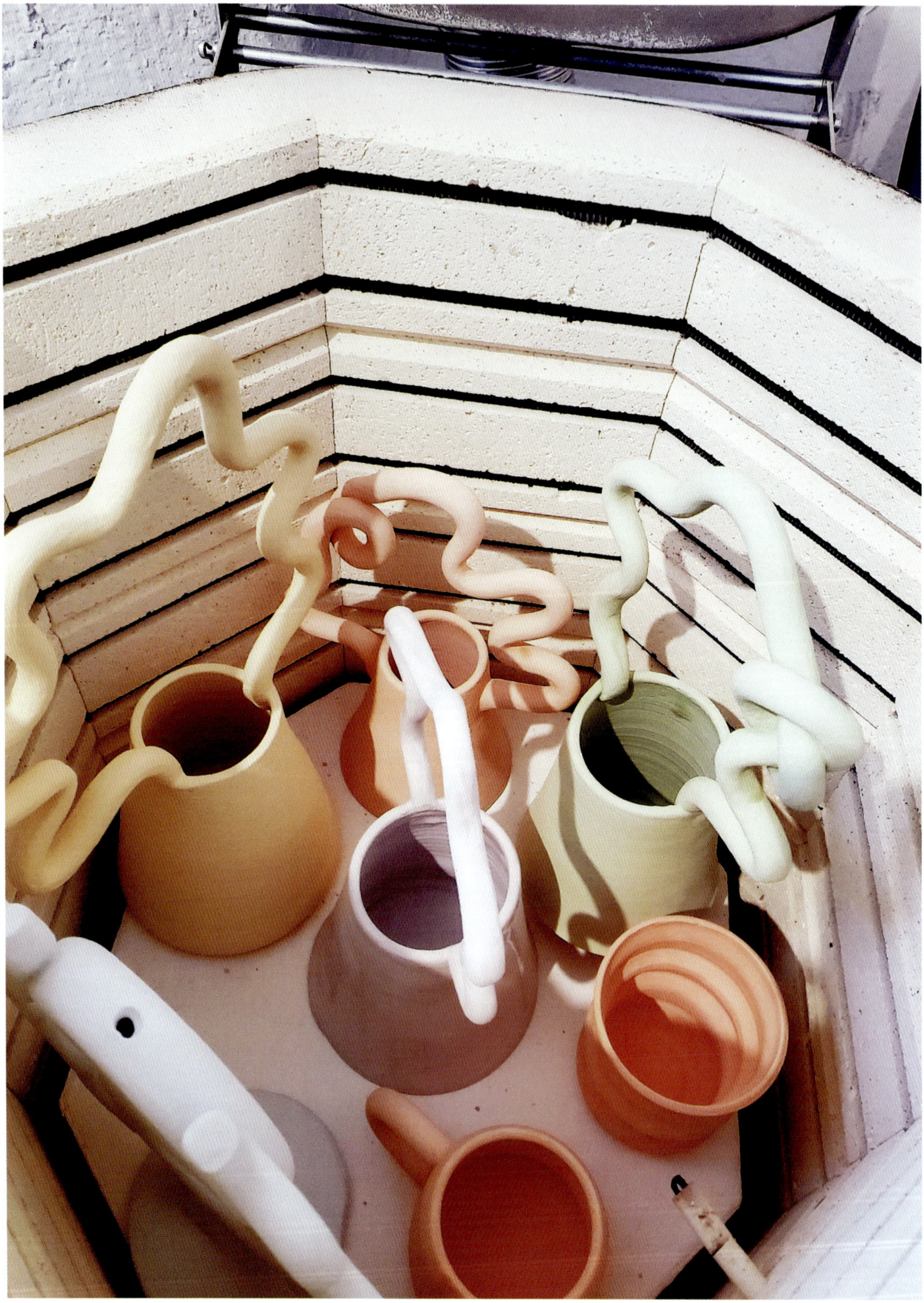

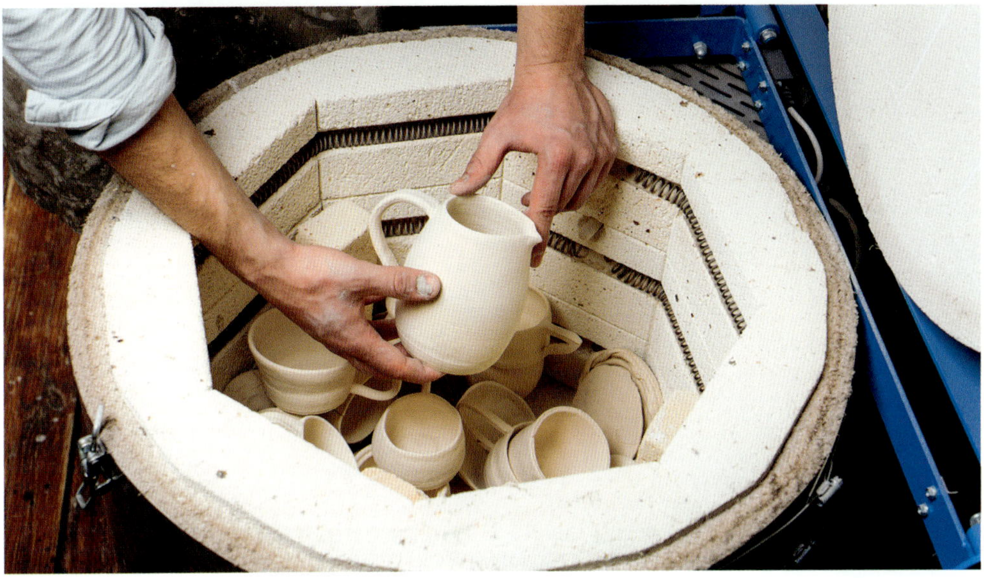

Electric Kilns

Electric kilns are reliable and easy to use and are commonly found in small and home studios. Skutt is a popular brand and is super user-friendly. They've even developed a touch screen kiln that helps you control your firings. Modern kilns usually have a digital screen, but older kilns still use physical cones to fire. With newer kilns you can set programs and hold temperatures at a certain point. For basic firing, electric kilns can be as easy to use as a kitchen oven. People often install these types of kilns in their basements and sheds. Proper ventilation is essential if you're considering getting a kiln as they produce harmful fumes when firing. Also, kilns have very specific electrical requirements. Hire a licensed electrician to install your kiln. Electric kilns can go all the way to cone 10; however, they usually fire only to cone 5 or 6.

There are many other ways of firing pottery, including gas firing, raku, pit, soda, wood, and more. If you're new to the process, I recommend sticking with electric kilns because of their reliability and consistency.

LOADING THE KILN

Loading the kiln can be like a game of Tetris. Because of how much energy the kiln takes to fire, potters try to get the most from each load. Because of this, there can be much maneuvering of pieces. Your kiln might be a top loader or front loader; either way the same rules of loading apply, as follows:

1. Start by assessing the pieces you intend to fire and organize them by height.

Note: Your pieces should never be loaded directly on the soft brick, which the floor of the kiln is made of. Place one-inch posts at the bottom on the soft brick then add the first shelf. The first shelf should sit on the one inch posts, raising it off the floor of the kiln. The reason we do this is for proper air circulation. Also, if you have a fume vent coming from the bottom, this will allow the fumes to exit. Remember, three posts per shelf—not four. If you're using half shelves, then you'll use six posts.

2 Before you start loading pieces onto your first shelf, first find the shortest post you can get away with without any pieces touching the shelf above it.

3 Load your pieces as close to each other as you can without touching each other or the shelf above. Place your posts in being mindful of even weight distribution. If glazed pieces touch, they will not only melt and stick together, but they will also create sharp and dangerous shards. Be mindful of the soft bricks that line the walls of the kiln and make sure the glazed pieces don't touch them. These bricks are delicate and with too much handling they can break and will need to be replaced.

4 If you think you're done and are ready to put in the next shelf, do a double check to make sure nothing is touching. Grab the next kiln shelf but remember to watch where you put your hands just in case there are any sharp pieces of glaze stuck to the kiln shelves. Watch out for the thermocouple when lowering the shelfs into the kiln. A thermocouple is a piece of the kiln that protrudes out into the loading area of the kiln. This is how the kiln measures temperature. Don't knock the thermocouple because if you break it, you won't be able to fire the kiln again until it is replaced.

5 Keep loading and adding posts and shelves until you're close to the top. If you have some tall pieces, you can always use half shelves that will allow you to load short things on one side and tall things on the other, making the most of the space in the kiln.

6 Close your lid. Set the kiln to the cone you want to fire. Kilns will likely include the option to set a preheating. This feature is great for bisque if you suspect there's any remaining moisture in your greenware. The kiln might also have the option to set an alarm for when the firing is done.

UNLOADING THE KILN

The kiln fires to thousands of degrees so it can take a half day to fire and then a full day to cool. Don't rush the cooling. Rushing the kiln to cool can cause thermal shock to your pieces, which can lead to cracking or crazing. I know we are all eager to see our finished pieces but be patient and wait until the kiln has dropped to 80 degrees. Some people open the peep holes to help the kiln cool faster, but keep in mind that the faster you cool the kiln the more you put your pieces at risk of breaking. After the cooling period is completed, unload your pieces and inspect them to make sure there are no sharp bits.

Here is what to do if there are sharp bits or pieces that are stuck together:

1 Grab safety glasses and a Dremel tool or sandpaper.

2 Sand the sharp bits to remove the bulk of the material.

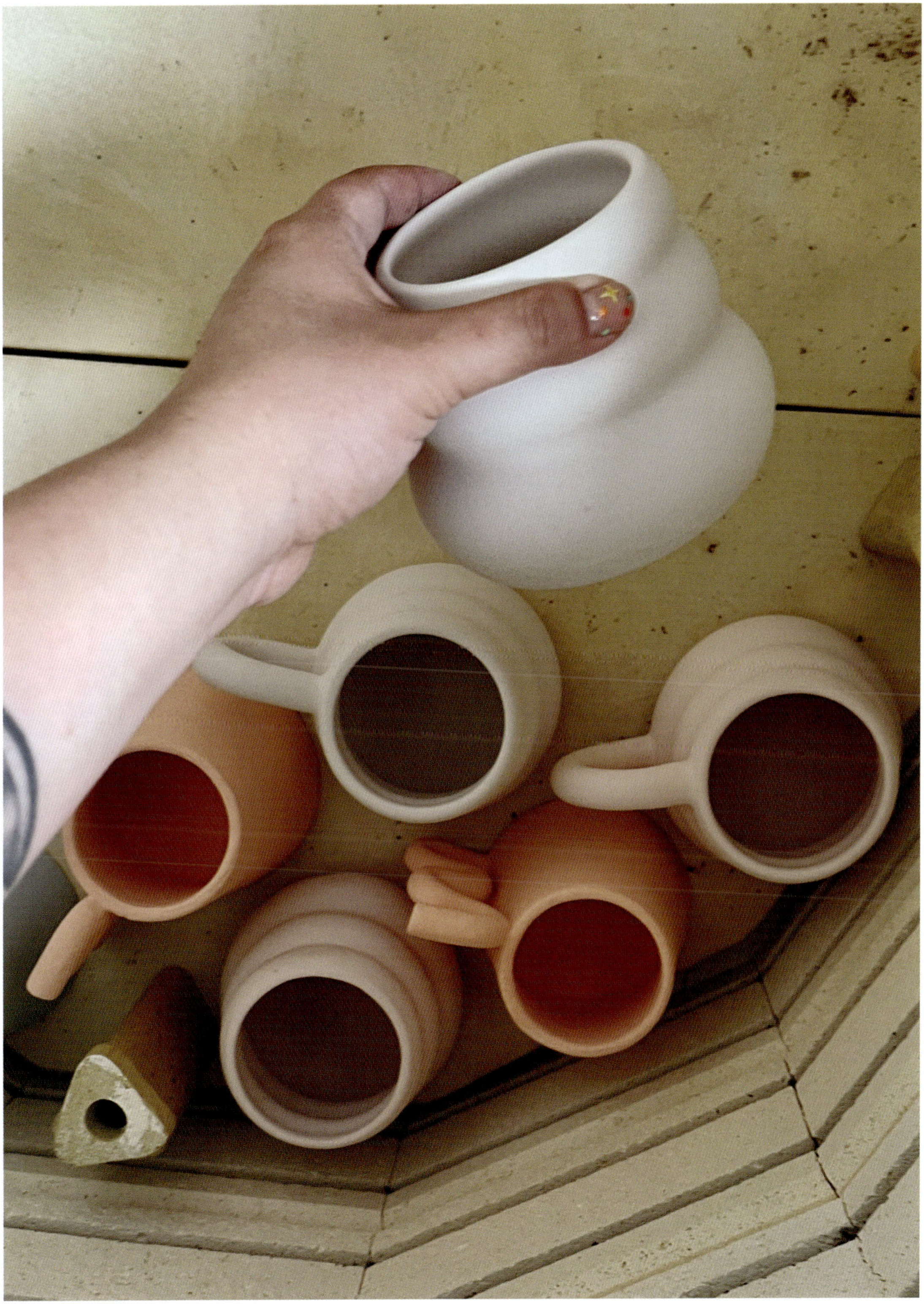

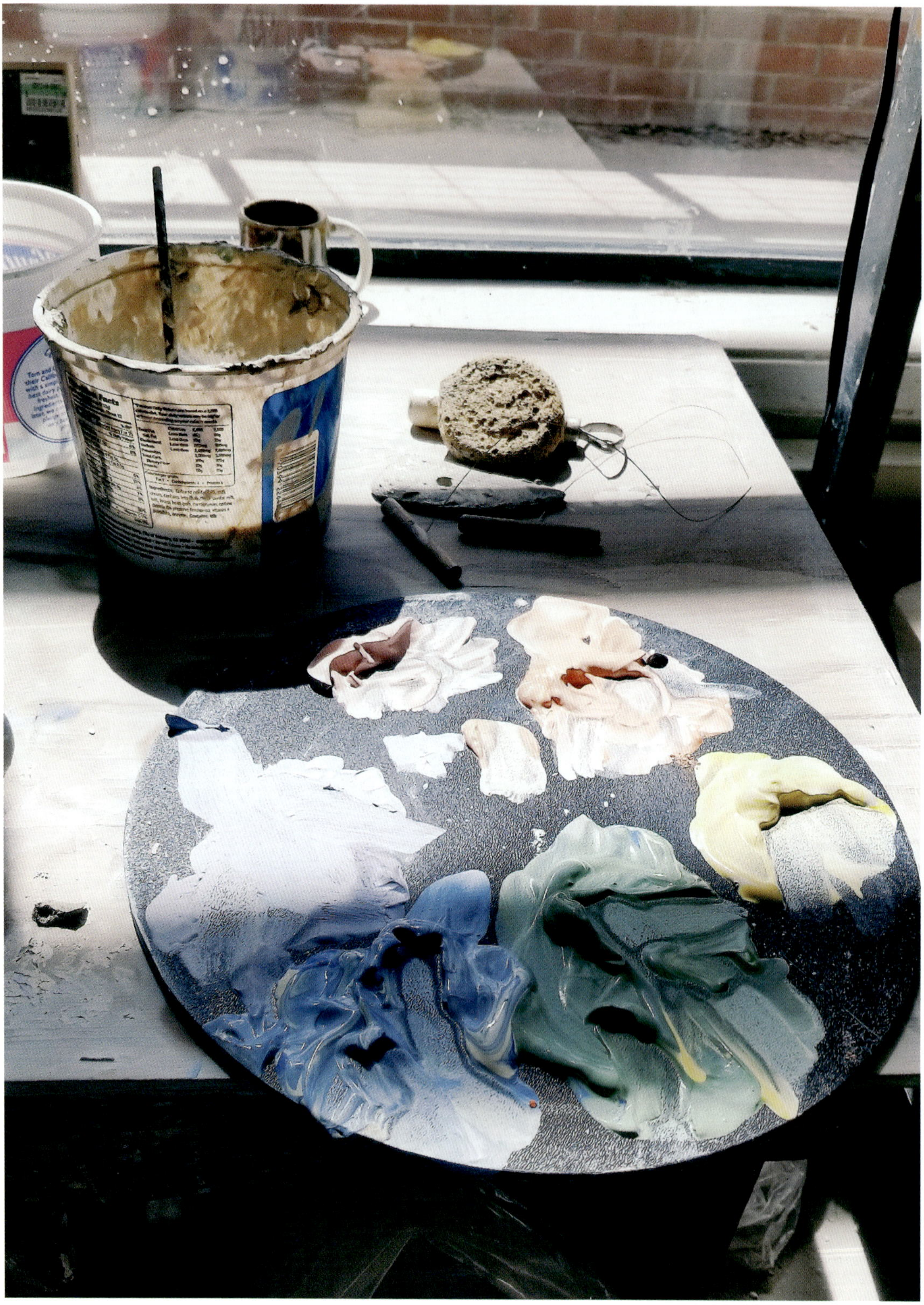

3. Add a touch of glaze to match the surrounding area.
4. Refire the piece so the glaze smooths out.

LOADING A BISQUE FIRING

Even though bisque firing happens before glaze firing, it's easier to learn glaze firing before bisque. However, loading a bisque is easier because the pieces can touch, which really opens up the possibilities. You can stack pieces together but remember the pieces will shrink when you're firing so make sure when stacking the pieces don't fit too tight because the rims might crack as they shrink around a piece or they'll get stuck together.

You can stack your pieces as high as you see fit. Some folks load a tumble stack, which basically means the kiln is packed to the brim with no organization.

NO KILN, NO PROBLEM!

Some ceramic supply shops and studios provide what is called a contract fire, meaning they'll fire items for you. It's a great option while you're learning without having to invest in a kiln. You will take your pieces to these shops as greenware for bisque firing and again for a glaze firing. The only downside is transporting greenware can be a little nerve-racking because the pieces are at the most delicate stage and can easily break during transport.

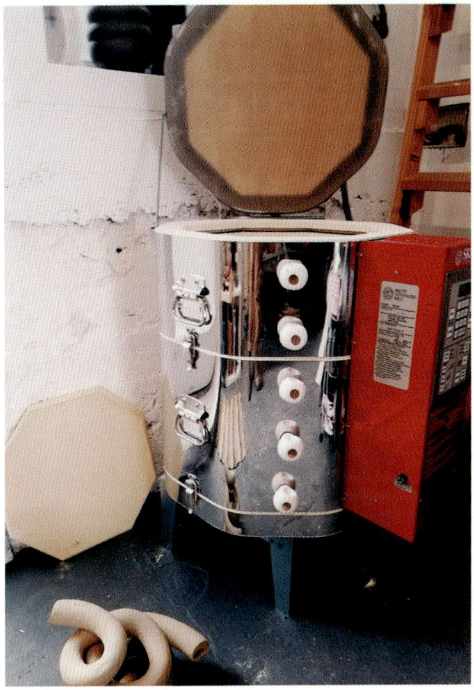

You can also become a member of a studio and use their equipment. This is a great option for learning through other ceramics artists, though can be a bit pricey.

Air-dry clay is a great option for you to experience clay without firings. This clay hardens when it dries and can be painted with acrylic paint. The only downside is there are limitations to things you can make that hold water or are food safe.

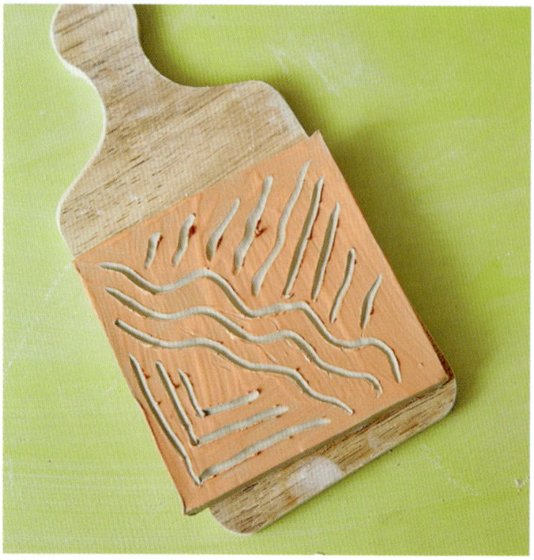

Sgraffito Tile

TOOLS

PAINTBRUSH
NEEDLE TOOL
PADDLE

Leather-hard clay can be decorated using the sgraffito technique.

1 First paint layers of slip on your piece until the coating is opaque **A** **B**.

2 Once the slip has settled for 15 minutes or so you can carve out decorations in the piece to reveal the underlying clay color **C** **D**.

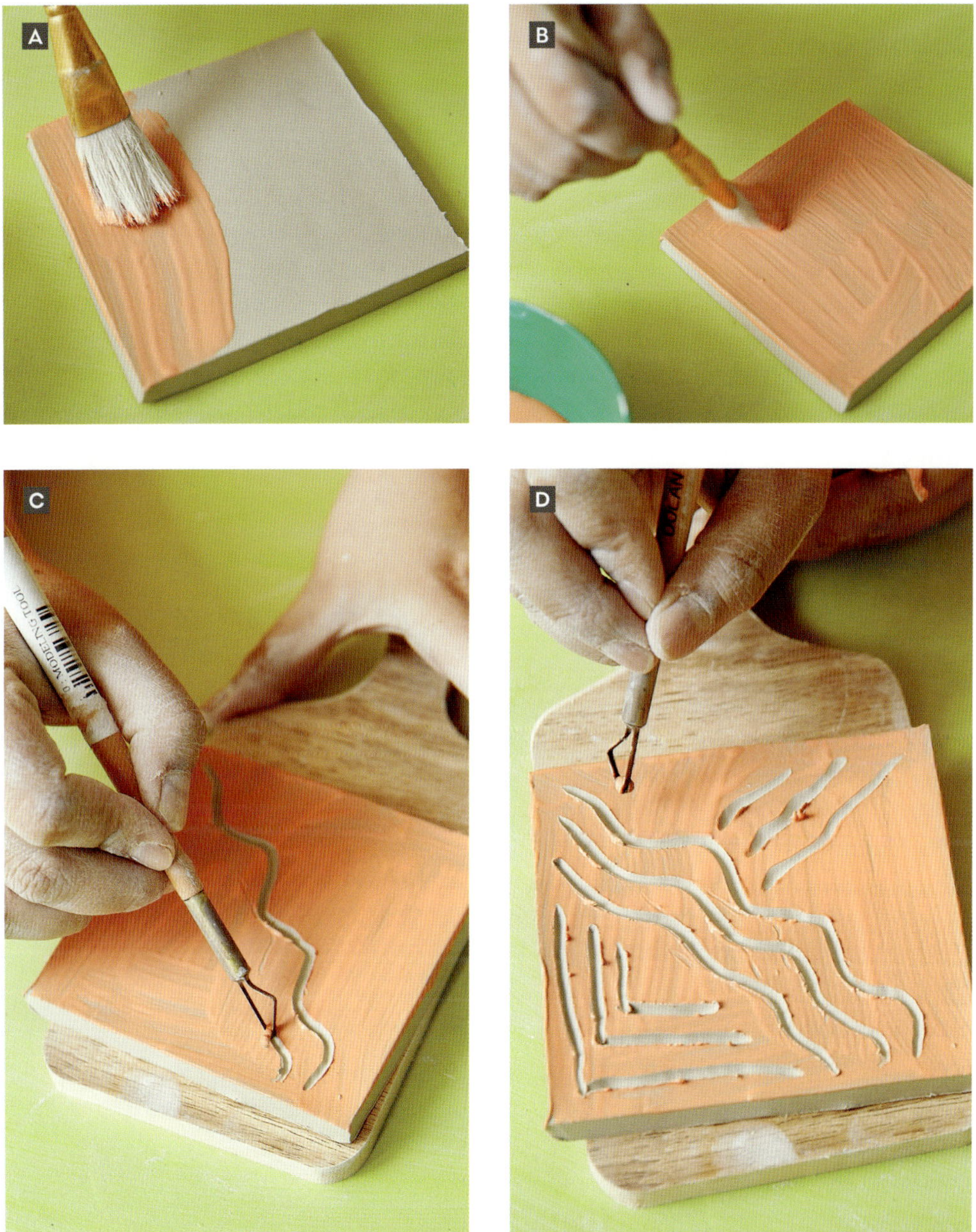
A
B
C
D

Bubble Glaze Bowl

Now that you have basic handbuilding skills you can start to work on having fun with them!

There are infinite ways to glaze but one of the most fun techniques is bubble glazing. What is bubble glazing? Bubble glazing is when you mix underglaze with water and dish soap to make a slurry that can be blown into bubbles and applied to a piece to create a unique effect.

TOOLS

BISQUE PIECE
WATER
DISH SOAP/HAND SOAP (NEEDS TO BUBBLE SO NO CASTILE SOAP)
UNDERGLAZE
BRUSH
DIPPABLE CLEAR GLAZE
SPONGE
DISPOSABLE STRAW

1 Have ready a piece of bisqueware you've created for this process **A**. Choose something large, nothing smaller than three inches or you might lose the effect.

2 Mix your slurry in a bowl with a brush making sure nothing clumps **B** **C**. The recipe is as follows:

3 TABLESPOONS OF WATER
3 DROPS OF DISH SOAP
1 TABLESPOON OF UNDERGLAZE

3 Grab your bisque piece, straw, and slurry. Put the piece on the table. Stand above your piece and put your straw in the slurry and start to blow bubbles but DON'T TILT THE BOWL **D**. It will be tempting to tilt it, but you might spill some of the slurry on your piece. The bubble method can be very subtle so if you spill you will be able to see it. Let the bubbles overflow out of the bowl and on to your piece and guide the bubbles so your piece is covered.

4 Allow the bubbles to pop on their own and you will start to see the pattern **E**. If you see very dark spots with no pattern, don't worry! Once it's glazed and fired you will be able to see the pattern more clearly.

5 Once the underglaze is completely dried, gather your clear dip glaze and dunk your piece for just one second. Make sure the underglaze is completely dried or it might bleed into your clear base and change the color. Wipe the glaze from the bottom of your piece.

6 Fire it up **F**! To make it safe for food make sure you use a food-safe glaze.

Note: You can layer two different colors of underglaze by doing one set of bubbles then allowing it to dry and then follow with another. Remember underglaze and glaze are very different.

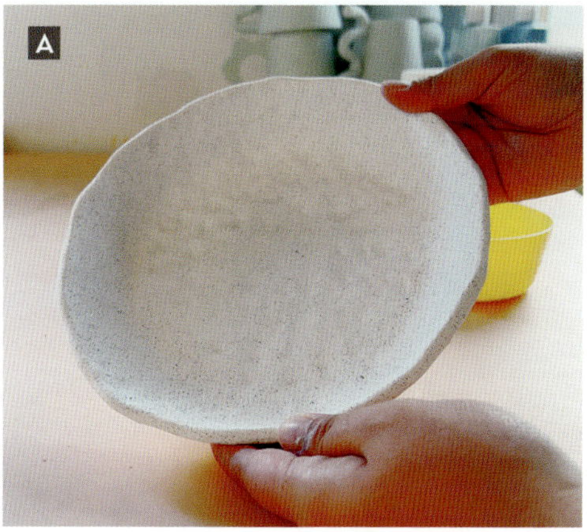
A

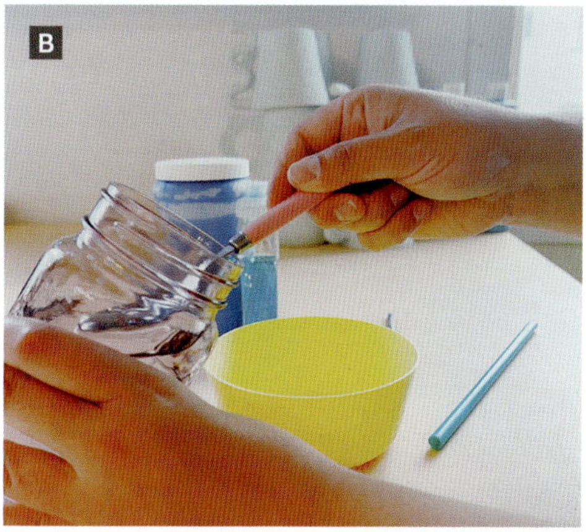
B

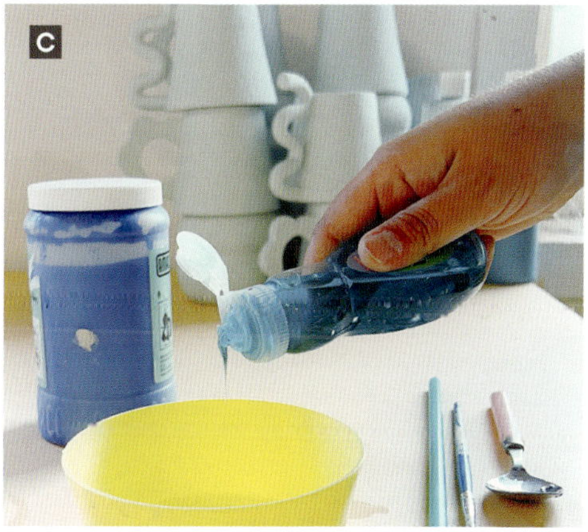
C

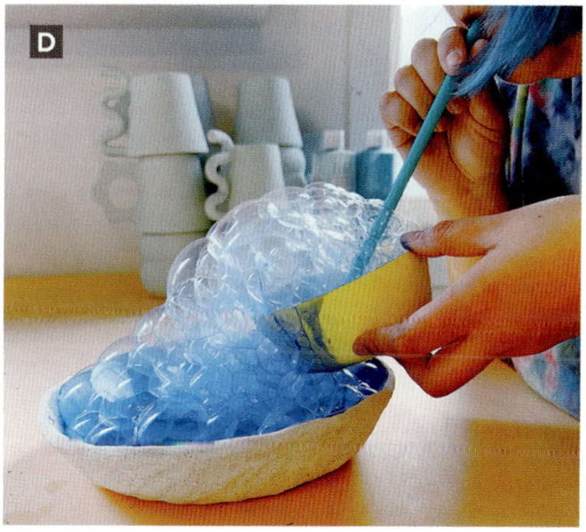
D

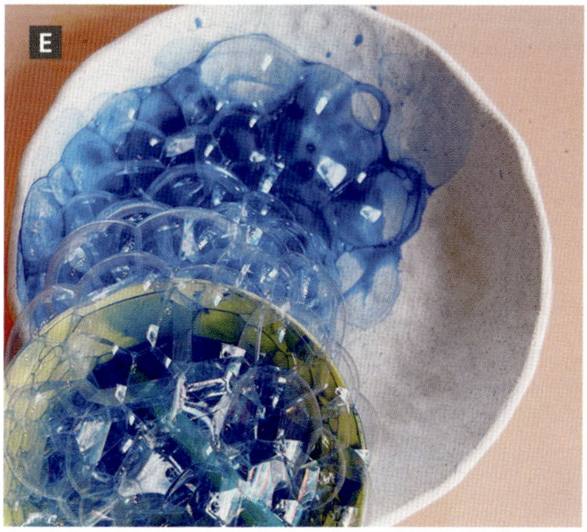
E

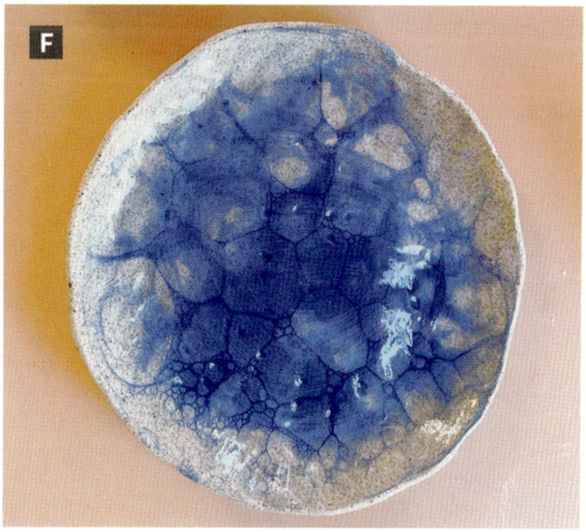
F

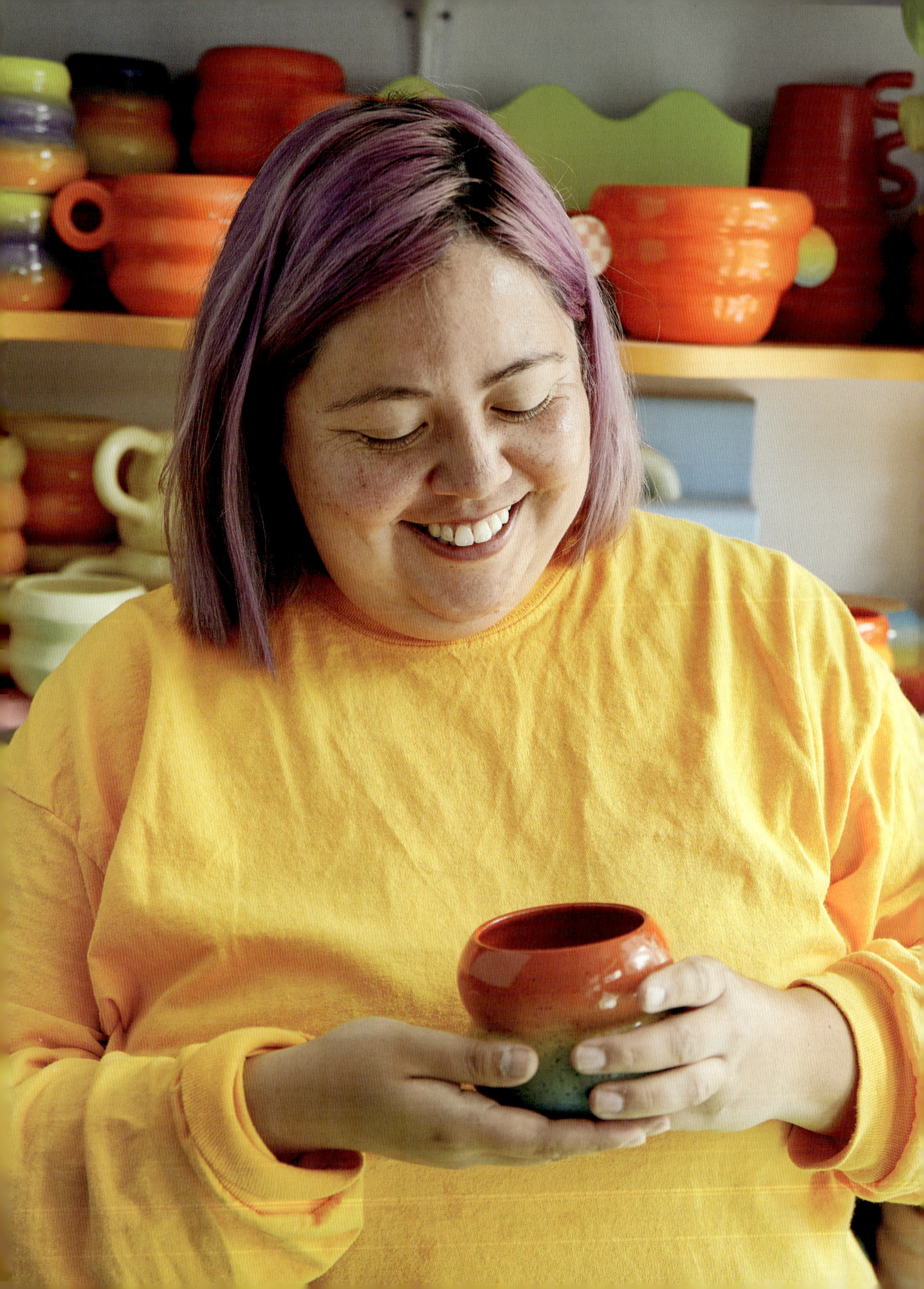

After the Making

CHAPTER 7

After the Making

In this last chapter, you will learn what to do after you're done with the making. Now that your piece is done, what do you do with the scrap clay? What do you do with your piece? How do you ship it if you'd like to sell it or give it as a gift? Read on for these details as well as space for reflecting on your creative journey.

Key Term

Wedging: When you handle the clay and compress and squeeze out the air bubbles.

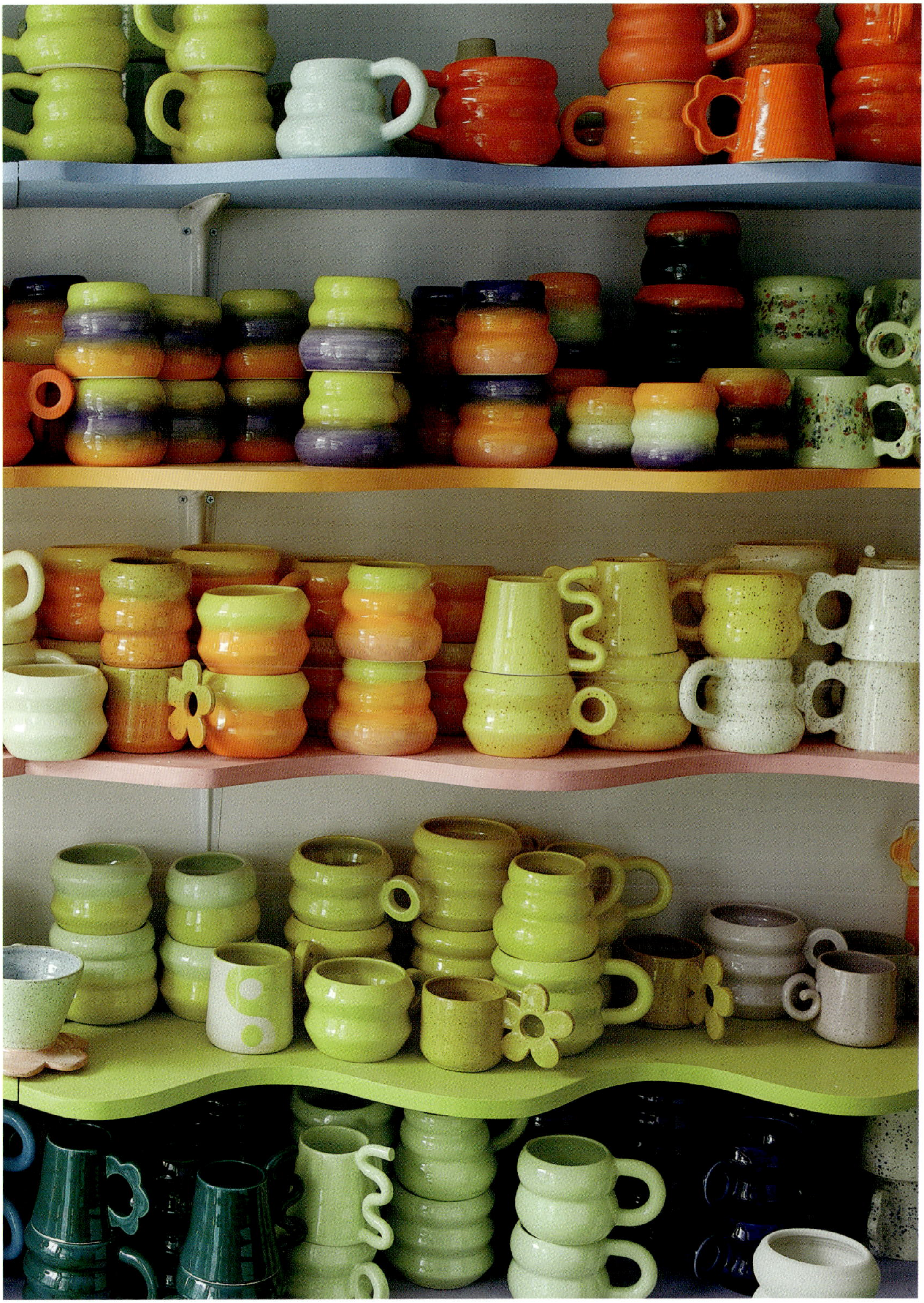

Repurposing Clay

The beautiful thing about clay is that it can be reused and rehydrated. The first thing to do is to determine the dryness of the clay.

1 If your clay is a slurry or slop, you will have to let it dry out a bit on a wedging table or plaster tabletop. Lay out the slop and poke holes throughout the clay to air it out. Check on the clay every half hour (depending on the temperature of the environment). The clay should be dry enough so it no longer sticks to the plaster or wedging table. Once it's at this stage it's time to wedge.

2 Start by cutting off a manageable piece for wedging, about the size of a head of cabbage. Then throw the clay down on the table and make a big ball.

3 Use your body weight to press and rock the clay without folding it over A B. You are compressing the clay down and once you get into the rhythm wedging can be fun. If you think you got all the air bubbles out cut the clay lump mid-way and see if there are any air bubbles.

4 If your clay is bone dry C, put all your dry scraps in a bucket or bowl D. Add water all the way to the top to make sure the clay bits are submerged E F. Wait an hour. You'll actually hear the water getting sopped up by the clay—it sounds like a high-pitched squeal. Let it set for an hour.

5 Once the hour is up, stir vigorously, preferably with a mixer attached to a power drill. Then follow the steps above on how to repurpose slurry or slop clay.

Note: If you've accidentally left your clay bag open, you can rehydrate it easily. Pour 8 ounces of water in the bag with the clay. Tie up the top and put the clay bag in a 5-gallon bucket. Now fill the bucket with water to the top of the clay bag and wait 24 hours. The next day you'll have a fresh bag of clay!

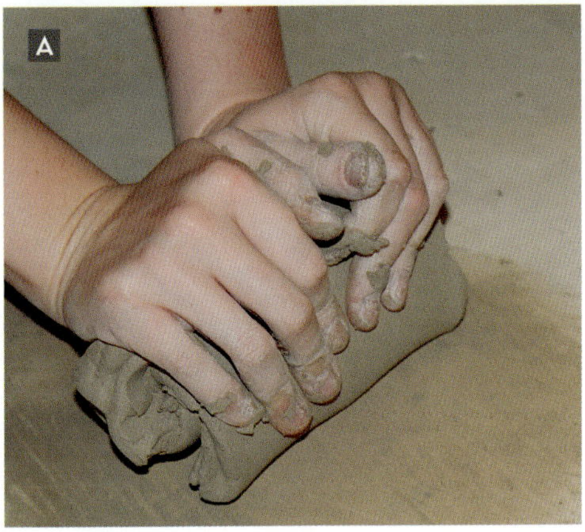
A

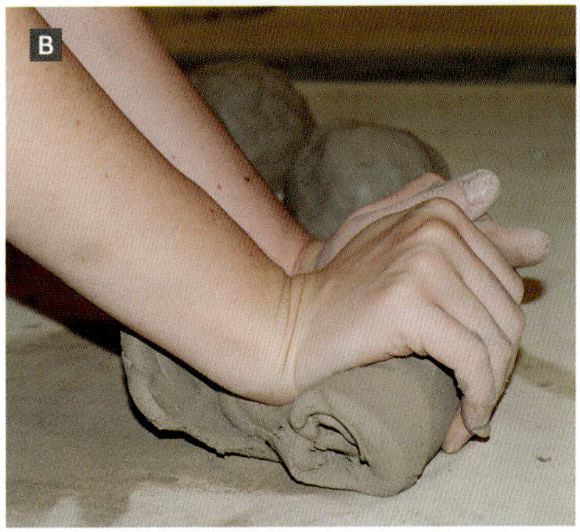
B

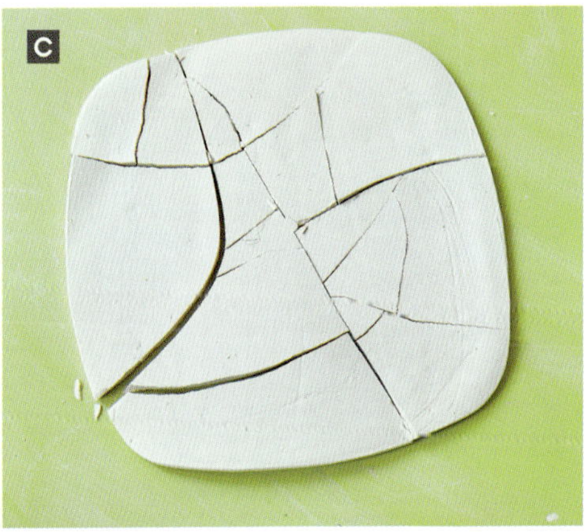
C

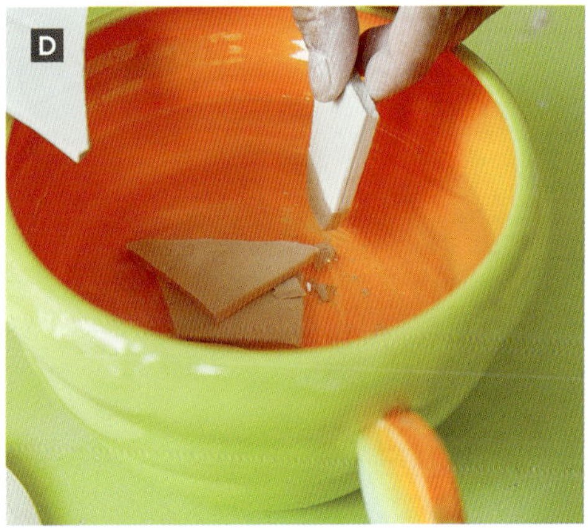
D

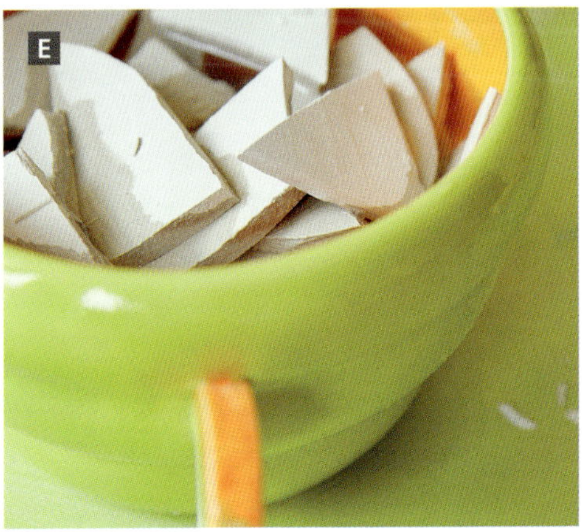
E

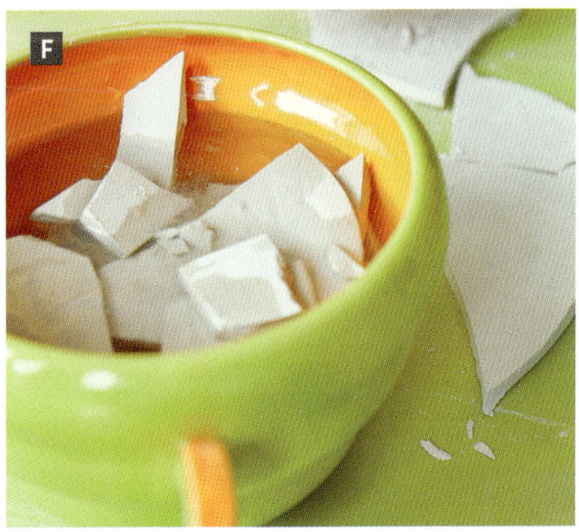
F

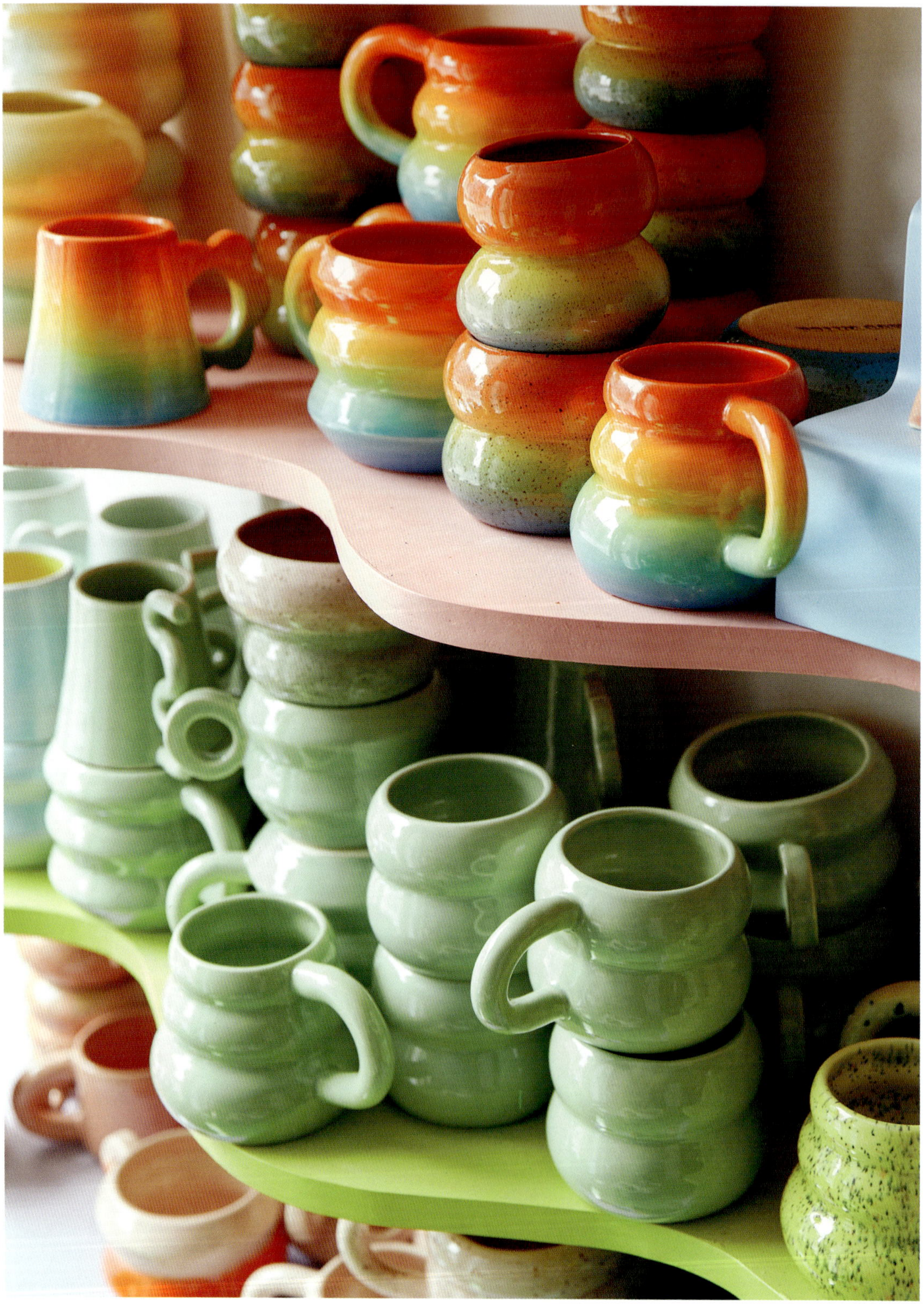

Shipping Your Art

Shipping delicate, breakable pottery can be tricky so this section should not be skipped.

1. Start by wrapping your piece in bubble wrap creating at least a one inch layer surrounding the entire piece. No part of the piece should show outside the bubble wrap.

2. Grab a sturdy box—we'll use one that is 6 × 6 × 6 inches in this example—and make sure the piece with the one inch covering of bubble wrap fits snuggly within the box. If there is any wiggle room, add more bubble wrap or some packing peanuts.

3. Tape the box shut and shake it to make sure there's no movement.

4. Next, you will double box your piece! This means you will use a second box that is one inch bigger on all sides than the first box. So, if you packed one mug in a 6 × 6 × 6-inch inner box, you'll need a second box that is a minimum of 8 × 8 × 8 inches. The general rule of thumb is that, at minimum, you need a one-inch barrier from the piece to the insides of the inner box and another one-inch barrier between the inner box to the outer box.

5. Now that you have the inner box packed, assemble the outer box and add a one-inch layer of packing peanuts at the bottom.

6. Place the inner box on top of the packing peanuts, centering it within the box, and then add peanuts around all four sides, filling the perimeter securely.

7. Pack the top with packing peanuts and then tape it shut. Shake the box to listen for movement. If there is no movement, it's ready to ship!

Displaying and Selling Your Pieces

Displaying Your Pieces: I recommend displaying only pieces you're proud of. They don't have to be perfect, and they don't have to be what was expected, they just need to be something that makes you smile when you walk past them. Some technical things to keep in mind are to be careful where you put your piece and make sure you use museum putty to adhere your piece to shelving in case of an earthquake or an accidental knock against the shelving.

Selling Your Art: There are many options and levels of selling your work. If you're a hobbyist, you can post to your personal work to social media and sell it to friends. If you want to grow bigger, creating a website is easier than it used to be, there are templates and all sorts of platforms that are very user-friendly. I recommend Shopify because it's very easy to use and works for all sizes of businesses.

CONCLUSION

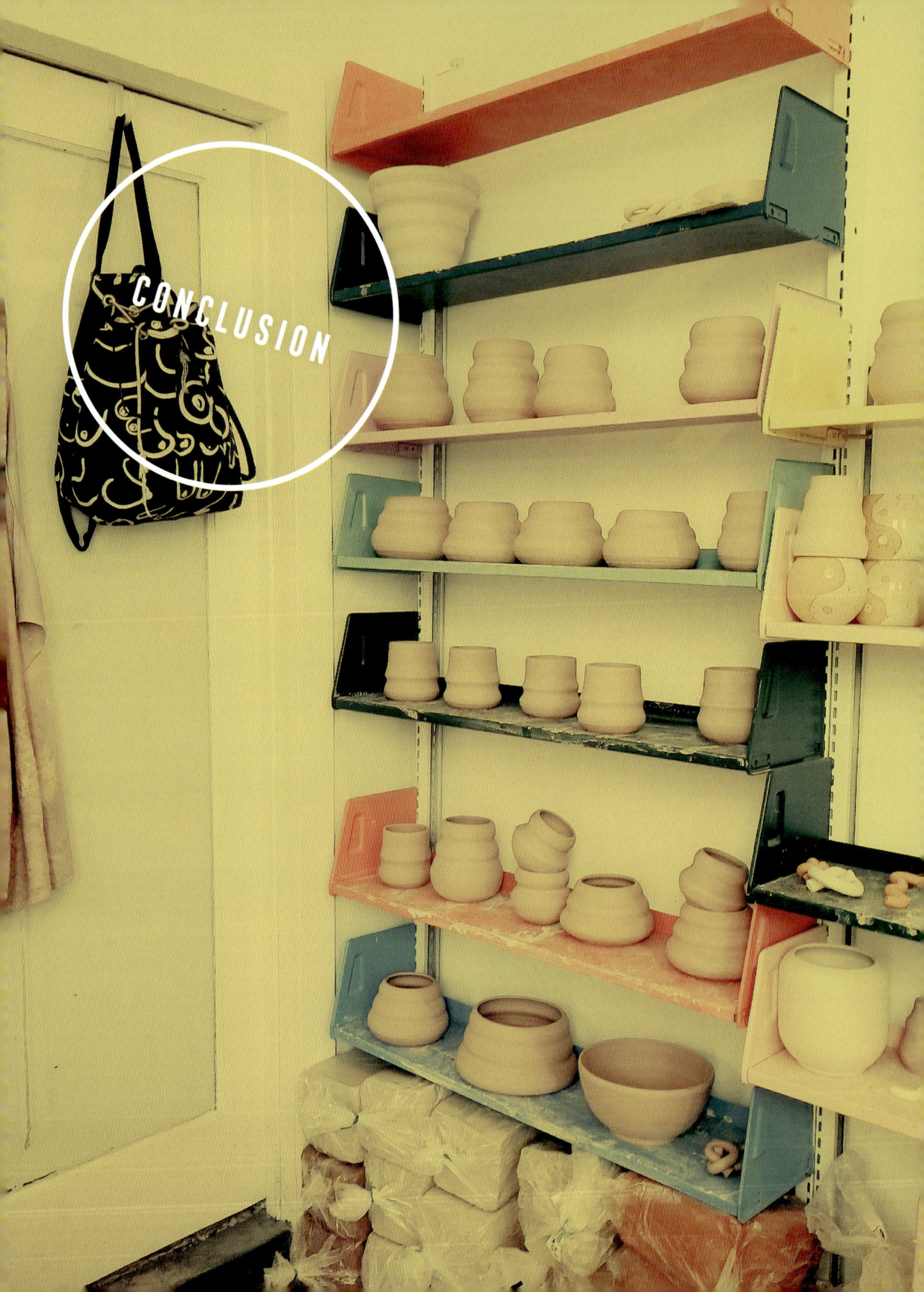

I have made so many mistakes throughout my ceramics career. I've had a kiln load explode, a kiln shelf crack, pieces melted to each other, melted down pieces, and ruined pieces; and with each experience I learned something new. Even after years of working with clay I still make mistakes and, if anything, **I have learned that ceramics is a humbling craft.** I'm hoping you take away from this book a general knowledge of ceramics as well as a better understanding on how to create.

Assess This Mess

Assess your progress. You can begin by asking yourself the following questions:

Did things turn out the way I expected?
Why or why not?
What can I do to change it?
What have I learned?
How did I manage my expectations?
How did I treat myself while learning?
How did I adapt when the unexpected happened?
What did I discover about my creative self?

RESOURCES

ClayPeople
www.claypeople.net

Blick Art Materials
www.dickblick.com

It's important to take notes on what works and why as well as what doesn't. You can also use these pages to document your progress. Draw out your pieces and break down how you will accomplish them. Maybe the base is wheel thrown and the top slab built? And maybe the handles are coil built? You can achieve the pottery of your dreams with the right planning!

Notes

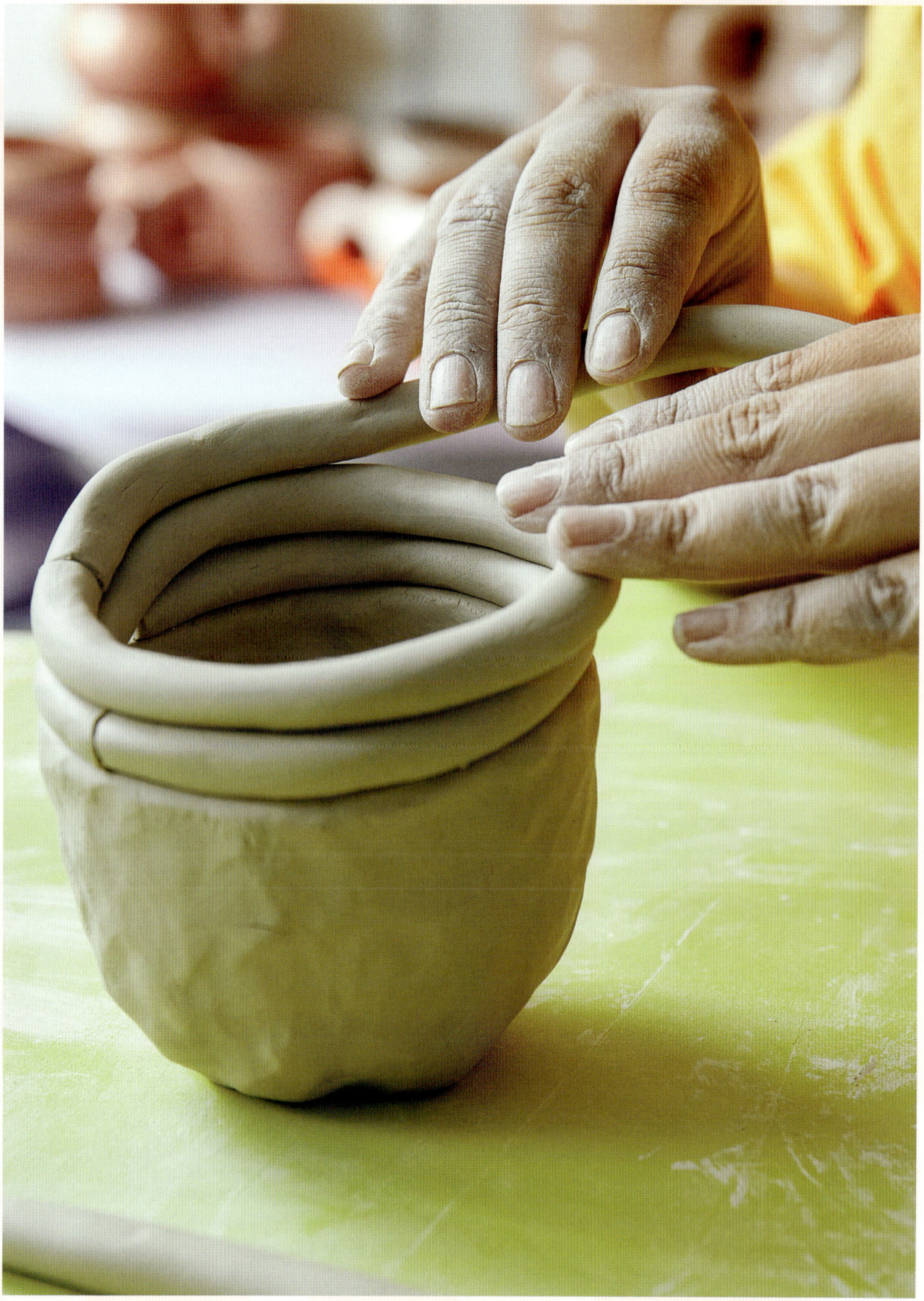

Notes

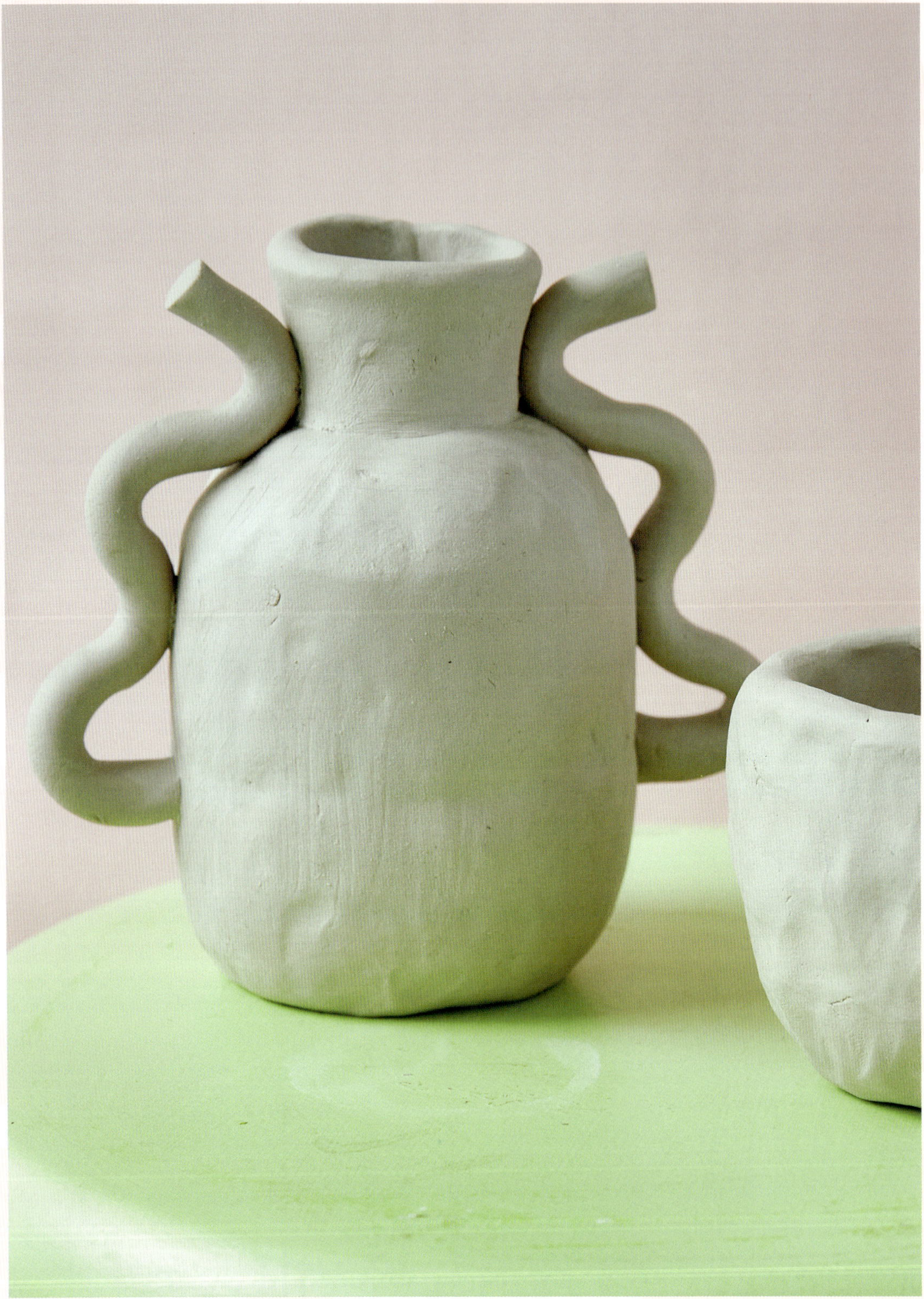

Notes

Notes

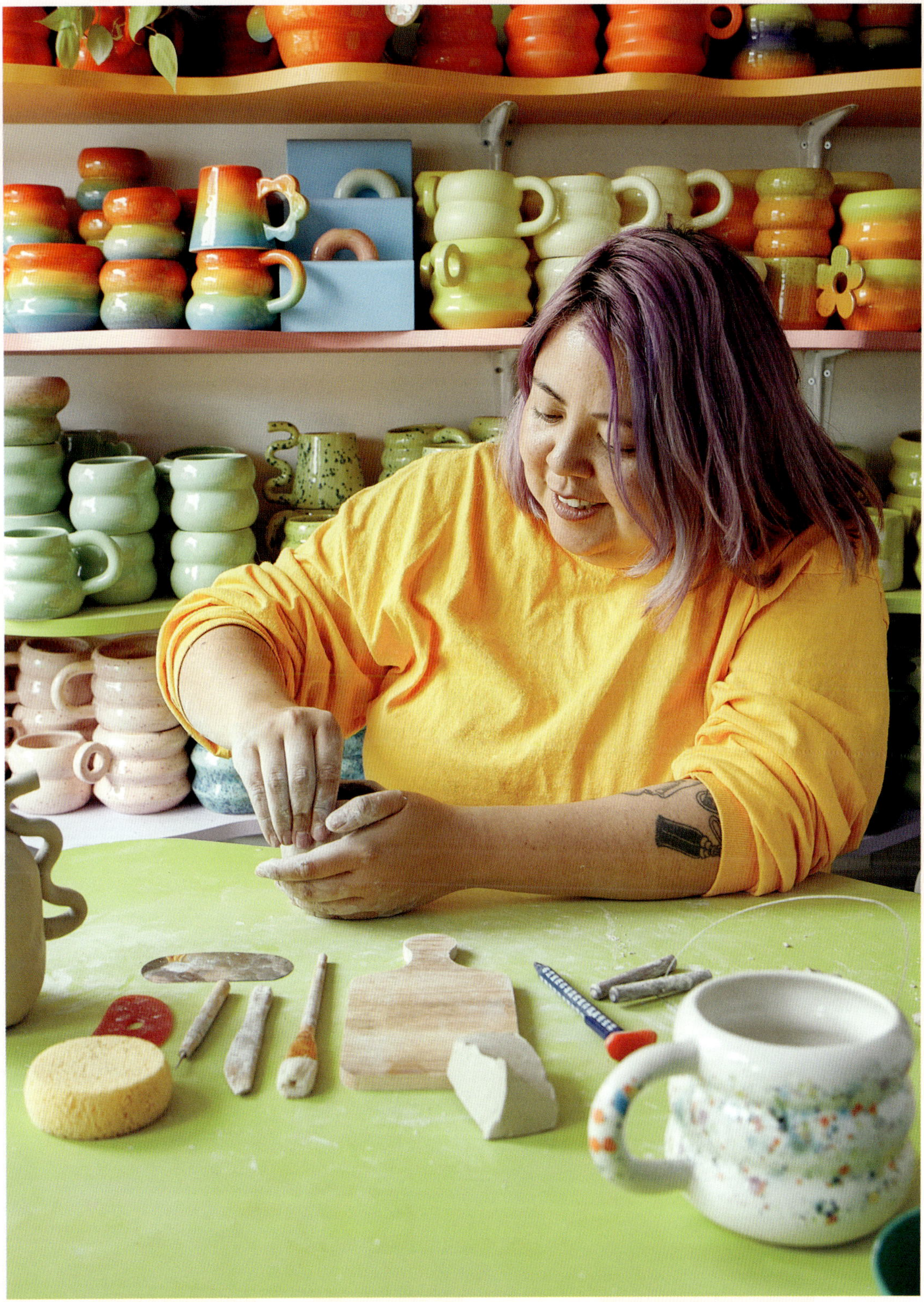

Notes

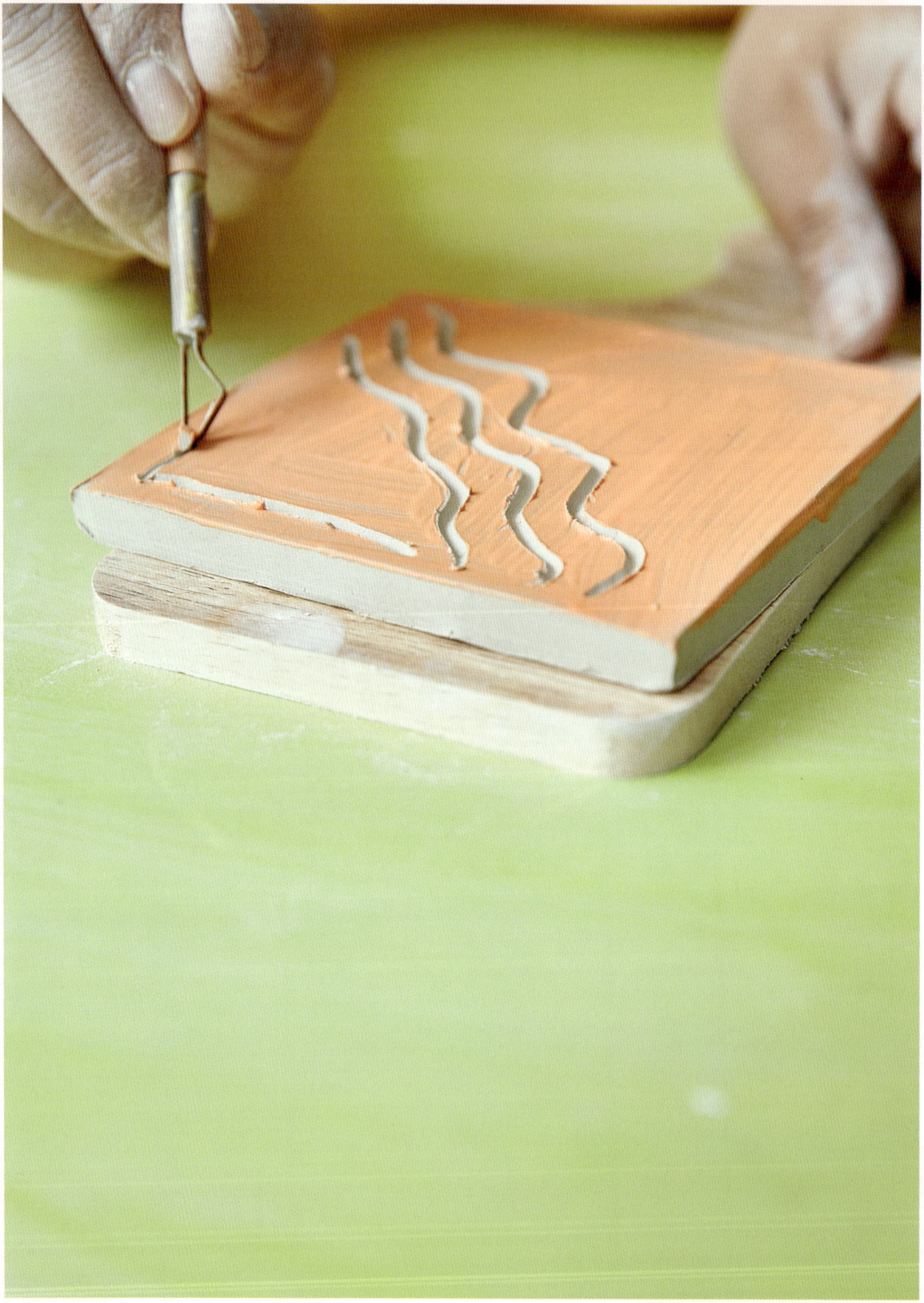

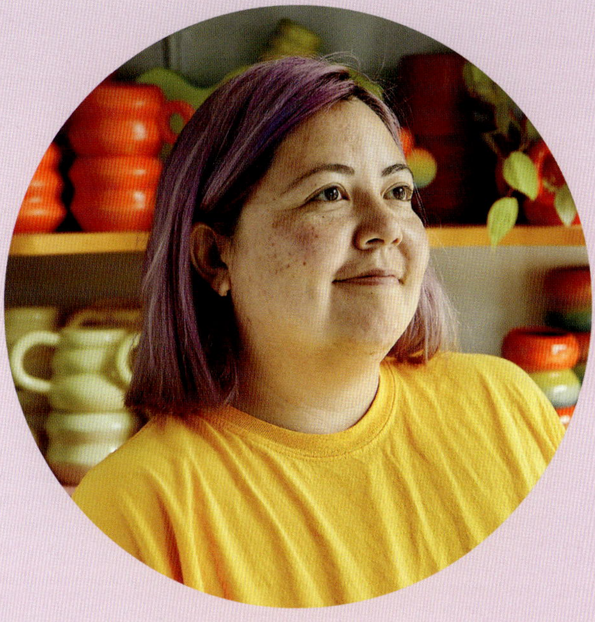

Viviana Matsuda (they/she) is a Japanese-Mexican clay artist and is the owner of Mud Witch, a small production pottery business located in San Francisco, CA. They started their journey in clay after their ceramic artist father passed away. While cleaning out their father's studio, Viviana found they were left with a bunch of clay supplies, so they decided to take a class at a local community college to work through their grief. Viviana quickly became hooked. They used clay as a stress reliever and found themselves in the studio five days a week throwing all sorts of shaped vessels. At the same time, Viviana was also learning about the body positive movement and the two interests combined to create their signature chubby-shaped mugs. Their apartment became full to the brim with pottery and so Vivi's partner suggested selling some pieces online so they would have some walking space and that was the start of the Mud Witch. They have been named one of *Sunset* magazine's 2019 Best of the West and one of *Dwell* magazine's "Designers on the Rise." They have also spoken on a panel discussing contemporary ceramics at Oakland Museum of California.

Explore their work and connect with them:

www.mudwitch.com
Instagram and TikTok @mud.witch

Check out their workshops and San Francisco retail space here: www.emotionpotion.net

Playful Pottery: The Mud Witch's Guide
to Creating Curvy, Colorful Ceramics
Viviana Matsuda

Editor: Kelly Reed
Project manager: Lisa Brazieal
Marketing coordinator: Katie Walker
Copyeditor: Joan Dixon
Design: Frances Baca
Cover photographs: Tommy Sullivan

ISBN: 978-1-68198-907-5
1st Edition (1st printing, January 2024)

Rocky Nook Inc.
1010 B Street, Suite 350
San Rafael, CA 94901
USA
www.rockynook.com

Distributed in the UK and Europe by Publishers Group UK
Distributed in the U.S. and all other territories by Ingram Publisher Services

Library of Congress Control Number: 2022937113

This book is printed on acid-free paper.
Printed in China.